U.S. Election 2016 NO COLLUSION?

—·—

An Unforgettable Severe Storm Our Historic Nightmare.

Jean Robert Revolus

CONTENTS

—·—

U.S. ELECTION 2016, NO COLLUSION?

Jean Robert Revolus

Dedication

I want to dedicate this book to my whole
family and my friends for supporting me
and making it possible. To the media
networks, Independents, DNC
members, some GOP Senators, a few
GOP Congressmen,
and some individuals from the
right-wing media who support the
reality of the

truth and who work so hard to make the fact available to the American people. This book is for those who deserve to know the truth to know what happened during the US Election in 2016. An unforgettable moment in American election
history.

— • —

ACKNOWLEDGMENT

I WANT TO ACKNOWLEDGE everyone who has assisted me with their knowledge while writing this book. More importantly, I would like to offer my sincere gratitude to you, the readers, for your willingness to explore the reality behind what we witness and experience.

— · —

ABOUT AUTHOR

J EAN ROBERT REVOLUS IS to be admired for his notable accomplishments that are nothing short of Extraordinary. As a devout Christian, a devoted husband, and a dedicated and enthusiastic father of four children, he says that God is front and center in his life. Jean Robert Revolus earned a degree in Business with an emphasis in Information Technology from Colorado Technical University.

In addition to his wide variety of experiences, Jean Robert is a well-rounded individual. He adeptly blends common sense and logic to navigate through the fields of Science, Religion, Philosophy, and Psychoanalysis. Throughout his career, Jean Robert has strived to establish himself as a credible author and a distinguished researcher.

A versatile and entrepreneurial individual, Jean Robert Revolus founded REVOLUS, LLC, a company specializing in social media marketing with automatic language translation to facilitate global communication. He serves as the company's lead project manager. He endeavors to do all this while passionately pursuing his career as a professional writer, a job he undertakes with enthusiasm and perseverance. One might presume that Jean Robert does not have much time to devote to any other pursuits besides his work. In reality, nothing could be further from the truth. His hobbies are limitless. They include singing, creative writing, and performing.

My humble opinion is that Jean Robert Revolus possesses some impressive talents; if he continues down this path, he will be a force to be reckoned with in the future. Besides his prolific writing style, he possesses a unique style that will make him a distinguished public figure of his time. Cain's Wife was neither his Sister nor his Relative; Women's Equality and the legitimacy of the 2016 presidential election are among his published writings.

PREFACE

THE US 2016 ELECTION is an absolute obstruct compared to other elections in the past years and probably for years to come. Politically, Morally, and even Socially. For politicians, this election was questionable. This event instigated doubts and admonished the political opponent to launch an investigation on the President to know if the President and his allies did not contribute to illegal activity to win this election.

Morally, The GOP brain is entirely corrupt, and no one needs to be a psychologist to see the reality behind the GOP brain. And Socially, most GOP Governors, senators, and members of Congress lack common sense when answering questions. They have one common goal, *"Keep the American people away from the truth."* and even consider the media as their worst enemy.

Collusion: Definitions and Meanings

Merriam-Webster's Dictionary as *"secret cooperation for an illegal or dishonest purpose."* However, *"a secret agreement for a fraudulent or illegal purpose; conspiracy"*. According to, collusion is *"a deceitful agreement or compact between two or more people, for the one party to bring an action against the other for some evil purpose, as to defraud a third party of his right"*.

Is it legal for a candidate to look for help from foreign countries to deceive the people of his country to win an election?

Some supporters believe that President Donald Trump is the fulfillment of the Bible; they strongly believe it is predicted in the Bible. I decided to ask a Doctorate Candidate in Theology, who is also a Political Analyst, Max Pierre. And according to him,

"There is no such information in the Bible related to President Trump, and he cannot support this account."

For those who support the Bible, there are six things that the Lord hates, seven that are an abomination to him: haughty eyes, a lying tongue, hands that shed innocent blood, a heart that devises wicked plans, feet that make haste to run to evil, a false witness who breathes out lies, and one who sows discord among brothers.

Moreover, according to **John 8:44**, you are of your father, the devil, and your will is to do your father's desires. He was a murderer from the beginning and had nothing to do with the truth because there is no truth in him. When he lies, he speaks out of his character, for he is a liar and the father of lies.

As everyone is conscious, the President is the Liar-in-Chief and cannot spend just half-hour without deceiving you. Now, it is for you to draw your conclusion at this point.

Some President's supporters believe that the President did not have any secret cooperation for an illegal action during the 2016 Election. However, if the President did not pledge an unlawful activity to convey him along with GOP Senators and Congressman to win the election. therefore, why those so many lies?

Why did they put so much effort into stopping the truth from being revealed?

The media had made many efforts to reveal the secret to the public. But so far, it has been unsuccessful. The President, along with the supporters of the GOP, even consider the media their worst enemy, which puzzles American society.

After Muller's Report which cleared the President, and his campaign of illegal secret cooperation activities with other foreign countries in other to deceive the American people, some analysts believe that the President is also guilty of Obstruction of Justice. However, to determine an Obstruction of Justice; there must be a first cause and an illegal action behind it, and through that cause, you can commit an Obstruction of Justice to prevent the public from clearly understanding your illicit activity.

Let's find out the foremost speculation, which leads to the Obstruction of Justice.

— • —

CONTENTS

P AGE LEFT BLANK INTENTIONALLY

CHAPTER ONE

— • —

THE ELECTION

THE U.S. ELECTION OF 2016 is regarded as the most surreal and unbelievable event in the history of America. From the most unusual nominees to the outrageous campaigns, from divisive controversies to the most unpredictable results; it was a rollercoaster ride. Nobody could even come close to guessing Trump's candidacy a year before the election, let alone predicting his success.

The 2016 Election was historic in many ways. It was a presidential contest between New Yorkers. Someone without any political or military experience was nominated too. For the first time, a female candidate ran for office, albeit a well-known politician.

The Unforgettable Election Night

Election night was a complete nail-biter as results started pouring in, and people sat glued to their screens. It was a night no one saw coming. In the early hours of November 9th, 2016, the celebrations started at the Trump Tower when the billionaire, entrepreneur, cum reality TV star, Donald J. Trump emerged triumphantly and became the 45th President of the United States of America. Supporters roared as the newly appointed President-elect of the US took the stage in New York City with his family to make his victory speech, after receiving the conceding call from his opponent, Hillary Clinton. Trump pledged: "I will be president for all of Americans, and this is so important to me." He added: "Now it is time for America to bind the wounds of division."

The Morning After – Shock, Mistrust & Anger

There's no denying the fact that Trump's victory was a shock for everyone, supporter or non-supporter, American or Non-American. However, it was especially devastating and utterly mortifying for the liberals. Videos of people crying their eyes out went viral over the internet as the news broke. It was a very, very long night for Democrats and their camps presented a sad sight. The night came to an end, but the morning held no ray of hope for liberals. It was as if the entire country was engulfed by a dense cloud of suspicion, mistrust, and apprehension.

Liberals shared the bleak sentiment as the prospect of having Trump as their President stared them in the face. They couldn't believe that the widely held US voters would make such a decision. They didn't know what or who to trust anymore. The country suddenly felt alien to them. About 1.3 million Citizens looked to the authorities to do something to fix it. To some, Trump was the champion of the new face of America, but many believed that having Trump in office was scary and a disgrace to women, minorities, immigrants, and people with disabilities.

Trump won, and this made liberals question the values of the nation. He had quite explicitly bragged about sexual harassment, mocked a disabled reporter, and tagged all Muslims as terrorists. Trump wanted to 'bomb every inch' of countries he thought 'deserved it,' African Americans were thrown out of his rallies, and he declared Mexicans as criminals and rapists.

Trump was unapologetic about his bigotry, and this enraged many people. People took to the streets at two in the morning, protesting against impending doom. They also felt guilty. Their thoughts started with *"if only..."* as if they have failed in fulfilling a considerable responsibility. Amanda Litman, a Clinton campaign worker, recounts the aftermath: *"I remember for months, every woman I saw on the street, I wanted to apologize to,"* She confessed, *"Little girls, little boys, I wanted to tell them, I'm so sorry this is the president you are going to grow up with."*

Women marched as a gesture of defiance against the newly elected leadership. Nine months later, they gathered in Detroit at the Women's Convention where they narrated their stories of election night, and how it transformed them.

Some liberals accepted that they hoped that President Trump might just come out of the full election mode and adopt a more controlled and balanced stance. However, they soon realized the naivety of their hopes.

Diane Russell, a former Maine legislator, and current governorship candidate recounted telling her friends, *"It's going to be really bad; I don't think you know what's coming. He means what he said."*

Soon the cat was out of the bag, and Donald Trump surrounded himself with conservatives. Trump continued to recklessly tweet and speak whatever came to his mind, uncensored. His inaugural address seemed to be full of the promises he knew, and everyone knew, he would not keep. *"This American carnage stops right here and stops right now,"* he vowed. There was no way he was going to step back from 'building the wall' or 'deporting the immigrants.' Trump's position on climate change and the Muslim ban was proof enough. His Twitter feuds, rants, and raw criticism against media houses remain unstoppable. The ghosts from this election continue to haunt the liberals to this day.

Election 2016 – Fact Check

On Tuesday, November 8th, 2016, the US observed its 58th quadrennial Presidential election. Republicans, Donald J. Trump and Mike Pence defeated Democrats, Hillary Clinton, and Tim Kaine. Trump was the first-ever candidate without any experience in politics or military service, whereas Clinton was the former Secretary of State.

Trump won the Electoral College with 306 electoral votes from 30 states in comparison to

Clinton's 227. Two Republican electors defected from Trump's camp, while five Democratic electors didn't vote for Clinton. That was the most significant political upset in modern US history since Clinton won every pre-election national poll and got 2.87 million more votes than her opponent. Trump was the fifth President to win office even after losing the popular vote. He is also the oldest and wealthiest President yet. He took charge of the President's Office on January 20, 2017. Clinton was a clear favorite, but still, she lost. Many experts compared Trump's success with that of Harry S. Truman in 1948. The polls conducted on election eve showed Clinton was expected to receive 52-53% votes whereas she got 51%. A two percent difference wasn't much of an upset honestly.

Statistics show that Republicans sealed their success and got 5% more votes in their active states. In swing states, they outperformed by 2% and failed to win in highly Democratic states. The better-than-expected results in Wisconsin,

Michigan, North Carolina, Pennsylvania, and several other states swung the elections in Republicans' favor. On January 6, 2017, an inquiry was initiated by the Government's Intelligence Agencies against the alleged Russian interference in the elections 2016.

Rust Belt States – Real Game Changers

The Rust Belt states such as Michigan, Ohio, Pennsylvania, and Wisconsin played a significant role in taking Trump to the Presidential office. There are 64 electoral votes in these four states. These states have been considered predominantly pro-Democratic. However, the Republicans did particularly well in the small cities and towns of these states. Michael Moore called it 'Our Rust Belt Brexit.'

These four blue states proved that there was nothing 'traditional' about this election. Until this election, these states remained loyal to the Democrats and did not follow in the footsteps of the rural, uneducated white population. The proof is Barack Obama's clean sweep in 2008, in which he bagged 53 out of 99 counties. In contrast to this, in 2016 Hillary failed to win any county except the six in Iowa.

We should keep in mind that all four of these states have not elected a single Democratic governor from 2010 to 2016. A valid reason for this surprise or instead shocks for Democrats is that the people of these states were unhappy, even angry. Clinton's support for NAFTA, TPP, and other trade policies had left the nations of the Upper Midwest in industrial turmoil. Voters also ignored Donald's big mouth when it came to his populist message. Trump's aggressive nationalism appealed to the people of Michigan, especially when Ford Motor Factory planned to shut down and shift to Mexico. He threatened the company that doing this would mean a 35% tariff on any cars that will sell to the US from Mexico. Trump's threat to Apple Inc. that he would force them to shift from China to America was also welcome.

It was a wake-up call for the Democrats who ignored the struggling, working class. Even if this class hated Trump, they seized this opportunity to send a message loud and clear: If you don't care for us, we don't care for you!

Hillary – Crooked?

Maybe it was not Trump that defeated Hillary. She defeated herself! A whopping 70% of the voters did not consider Hillary honest and trustworthy. They thought Hillary is, as per Trump, crooked. She represented the classic model of the old, rotten political system. All she wanted was to get elected, and she was ready to do anything for it. She behaved like a pendulum on many issues. She supported and officiated a gay marriage, and at the same time, had an anti-gay-marriage stance. The truth is that the youth of the country didn't like her. Millennials generally, and young women especially dislike Clinton. Even though Hillary and the women of her age group have struggled a lot for the women of today's generation, Hillary had somehow failed to connect with them. Remember the enthusiasm and motivation of Democrats and independent voters when they chose Obama as their President? That was completely missing from the election 2016. The voters were not excited to vote for her the way they would have been if Bernie Sanders was running.

The scandals, controversies, and investigations surrounding Hillary also drove the crowd away from her. FBI was investigating her until just two days before voting. The timing was unfortunate, although the research reached a dead end. The leaked emails had undoubtedly tarnished her image publicly, and she didn't do anything substantial to make up for it.

In 1992, Bill Clinton's advisor James Carville coined a phrase: *"It's the economy, stupid,"* In 2016, she failed to address this significant issue. Both the candidates had their fair share of haters. But it all depended on getting the people out of their houses and voting. Trump managed to do just that.

To Vote or Not To Vote, That Is the Question

Another thing that turned the game in Trump's favor was the votes from Bernie's supporters. There was no way they were voting for Clinton, and Trump was the only other choice that they had. The Cooperative Congressional Election Study conducted an election survey with 64,600 people, and the statistics showed that 12% of Bernie Sanders' supporters voted for Trump.

The people who wanted to vote for Bernie decided to either vote for Trump or not vote at all. However, the voters who reluctantly voted for Hillary were called *"depressed voters,"* which means that the voters did not find a reason to support her.

Brian Schaffner is a political science professor at the University of Massachusetts, and he presented the numbers to prove, that more than one in 10 of those who voted in the primaries for the progressive Sanders ended up voting for the Republicans in the general election, rather than for the Democratic candidate, Hillary Clinton.

Let's Shake Things Up

According to a study by Pew, Donald Trump and Hillary Clinton were the least popular nominees among Americans in the history of presidential elections. Honestly, this should not surprise anyone as both the candidates had to participate in dirty, intrinsic party politics and had sufficient opposition from within. The stats suggest that Clinton was the most unpopular nominee running with a Democratic ticket since 1992 – when Bill Clinton, her husband, was the most disliked because of the Gennifer Flowers sex scandal.

On the other hand, Republicans were not particularly happy to nominate Trump as their President, too. Republicans were even less thrilled to vote for Trump than they were when George H.W

Bush betrayed them by going back on his '*no new taxes*' pledge. Since 1992, if more than 50% of any party's voters disliked their candidate, he/she lost. In 2016, this trend ended. Voters were not happy with their nominees, but they could not just turn a deaf ear to the election campaigns. Americans were excited to vote and thought the stakes were higher than before.

Voting and choosing their President makes the Americans feel their freedom. That gives them the power to shake things up. In the 90s, something similar happened. Jesse Ventura was chosen as the governor by the people of Minnesota. The voters were not stupid; neither did they think he was politically trained. They picked him because they could. The population of Minnesota is smart and dark-humored – a lethal combination. It was a joke they played to slap the corrupt political system in the face. The same thing probably happened in Trump's case.

In 2008, Barack Obama sold the idea of change. In 2016, people saw Trump as their change. Approximately 80% of Americans thought that choosing Trump would shake things up in DC, but only 33% thought the move would be for the betterment. Also, that is the exact reason why one should never underestimate the voter's ability to challenge the system. Choosing Trump was also an expression of anger toward the crippled political system. The majority of Trump's voters did not do it in his support or because they loved his colossal ego, bigotry, or immaturity. They voted for him as revenge.

Bimodal Divide in Voting Patterns

The presidential election of 2016 demonstrated two unique patterns that highlight the growing disparity in the Electoral College system in the U.S. Let us look at the statistics:

- Donald Trump won with a considerable

margin in the Electoral College by bagging 306 electoral votes.

- Hillary Clinton got the maximum *"popular votes"*, 2.8 million votes over Donald Trump.

The question is why there was such an incongruity between the percentage of the Electoral College votes won by the two candidates, and the percentage of the popular vote won by them. The Economist, in an article, proposed that America's Electoral College system gives the Republicans an edge over the Democrats.

Their statistical model showed that even though Democrats win 99.9% of the popular vote, Republicans have a 30% chance of being re-elected for another term. The reason for this discrepancy was that the Democrats won the seats with huge margins in states with a more significant population. They got a higher number of popular votes, but the number of seats remained limited. Whereas, Republicans won a higher number of districts even if with narrow margins. In 2016, the Democratic candidates who defeated the Republican nominees did this with an average of 67.4% of votes. In comparison, Republicans won with an average of 63.8%. This clear bimodal divide is the result of the imbalance in population and geographic area. Also, urban areas have a more significant Democratic population. That contributed to Trump's historic win in 2016.

Maps that displayed vote tallies by geographic area were misleading because this discrepancy of population vs. geographic area in voting patterns could better observe in cartograms that show regional vote tallies weighted by population density.

"Large, densely populated Democrat cities (NYC, Chicago, LA) do not and should not speak for the rest of our country?" That was the question raised by Allen B. West. The answer to this can be subjective, but we can reach a few conclusions:

CHAPTER TWO

— ⋅ —

COLLUSION

What is Collusion?

Collusion

- Presidential elections are all about state-wide votes, and the number of votes won from individual counties or cities is irrelevant.

- The President of the U.S. is the representative of the country as a whole and not a particular geographic area. He is accountable for the well-being of ALL Americans.

- To resolve this *"bimodal divide,"* a bicameral system was set up over 200 years ago. This legislative branch of the U.S. federal government was made to ensure that the *"House of Representatives"* represents states based on population, and the Senate portrays all states, irrespective of their population.

Noun Secret or illegal cooperation or conspiracy to deceive others.

Considering the definition mentioned above of the term *"Collusion,"* it becomes clear that the word is used to describe cooperation in a harmful or illegal manner. As defined in the dictionary, collusion refers to any activity which includes forming an association or an alliance, which has a primary objective of finding ways to cheat on other individuals or the entire system.

An act of collusion might not be entirely illegal, but it involves such doings which further turn it into a conspiracy. In the court of law, sometimes it becomes quite challenging to prove a case of collusion. Most of the cases may show that some unethical activity did take place, but nothing illegal occurred since it is challenging to find evidence. The previous elections represent the perfect case of collusion, and that is precisely what all the fuss is about; *whether it is collusion or crime.*

Donald J. Trump
@realDonaldTrump

"Where's the Collusion? They made up a phony crime called Collusion, and when there was no Collusion, they say there was Obstruction (of a phony crime that never existed). If you FIGHT BACK or say anything bad about the Rigged Witch Hunt, they scream Obstruction!"

Since the U.S. Election 2016, the word *"Collusion"* has been so extensively used by political experts and TV hosts that the general public was curious to know what it is. Proof of this claim could be the 1800% hike in people searching for its meaning on Merriam-Webster. After Special Counsel Robert Mueller's investigation, people wanted to know all about the term and what it implies.

Even though President Trump defines it as a *"phony crime"* in his tweets, the real idea behind the coined word can only come from the antitrust laws of the country. The word itself does not have any technical or legal connotations, but it refers to secret agreements, conspiracy, and cooperation with illegal or deceitful intentions. It has been used previously to imply the secret deal between different parties to meddle with fair competition by deception, lies, rumors, and fraud. It was used in economic circles when companies tried to divide a market, limit opportunities; or got involved in fixing prices.

However, the term became a buzzword internationally after the U.S. Elections in 2016. The unbelievable outcome of the election was enough to make people suspicious about the possible ties between the Trump camp and Russia. The newspapers printed *"Collusion"* in their headlines, and it soon became synonymous with the alleged collaboration between both parties for supporting his election campaign and helping him bag the victory.

Trump Campaign and Collusion Allegations

The Trump-Russia affair has remained in the headlines for the past two years. The conflict and controversy associated with Trump's presidential campaign have seeped into the present administration too. To understand the recent developments; it is crucial to learn about what happened and how. It all started with a series of cyber-attacks on the Democratic candidate, Hillary

Clinton, in which her classified emails got leaked and altered. She became a victim of fake news stories that were planted on social media to tip the scales in Trump's favor. US intelligence agencies concluded in 2016 that Russia was behind these attacks, and state-authorized hackers carried out the attack that seemingly boosted the candidacy of Donald Trump. It resulted in chaos in the political and social circles of the country.

On September 22, 2016, United States Congress members publicly announced Russia's interference in the recent elections. The United States Intelligence later confirmed the announcement on October 7, 2016. After three months, the Director of National Intelligence reaffirmed and elaborated this claim. It revealed that the orders for the attacks came directly from Russian President Vladimir Putin's office. It seemed Putin wanted Trump to win and Hillary to lose, and he influenced the elections by fueling the propaganda against the Democratic candidate.

However, Russia was not the only player in this game. Trump's campaign team was allegedly conspiring with foreign agents too to defeat their opponent. Donald Trump was accused of colluding with Russia. Although both presidents denied all such allegations, and Trump even went on to call it *"the greatest political witch hunt in history,"* the situation required a probe to get the facts and examine them. That called for a Special Counsel's investigation, and that is where former FBI director Robert Mueller entered the picture. The investigation began in May 2017, and he reported his findings in March 2019.

Is Collusion a Crime?

Gone are the days when Rudolph Giuliani was called brave for his fight against crime as a US attorney or when he was loved for being valiant as the mayor of New York after the 9/11 incident. In recent times, Rudy has emerged as a defender of Donald Trump.

"I have been sitting here looking in the federal code trying to find collusion as a crime... Collusion is not a crime." said Rudy Giuliani when he appeared on *"Fox and Friends"* as Trump's lawyer. His remarks on Mueller's report sounded utterly ludicrous.

In Giuliani's perspective, even if Trump was involved in collusion with Russia, it was entirely correct since the legal system does not define collusion as a legal crime. He defended his client by telling the viewers that Trump was not wrong in seeking help from the Russians to get the upper hand in the elections. He also proudly declared: *"it was over with by the time of the election."* He repeated his comments on ABC when asked about Michael Cohen (Trump's former attorney replaced by Giuliani), and the information he has provided for the investigation against the collusion. He went one step ahead and called Cohen, *"pathetic."*

He also claimed that the President had no idea about the notorious meet-up between Trump Jr. and Russians at Trump Tower during the 2016 presidential election campaign. He further added, *"But if Roger Stone gave anyone a heads up about WikiLeaks leaks, that is not a crime."* That motivated the President, who then took to Twitter (as usual) to reiterate the point. The tweet read: *"Collusion is not a crime, but that does not matter because there was No Collusion (except by Crooked Hillary and the Democrats)!"*

The Cries of Witch-Hunting

The truth of Russians meddling with our election with inside help was sold under the name *"Collusion,"* so feverishly that Trump's attorney now has a chance to spread doubts regarding the legal connotation of the term. Yes, no crime called 'collusion' exists in US legislation, but it is just a matter of terminology. For instance, if a person kills someone with a gun and is accused of shooting, there is no reason to say "no, shooting is not a crime, homicide is."

Trump and Rudy Giuliani's narrative that collusion is not a crime, creates an air of confusion and supports their cries of witch-hunting. Trump calls it the greatest witch hunt in history. In light of this investigation, it is evident that Trump has several business links with Russians. These ties are older than his presidential candidacy. It has been a well-known fact that he had previously befriended crooks and criminals and hired them as advisers as well. For example, the chairman of his campaign has been sent to prison for financial crimes. Trump fears impeachment, and that is why he is making sure that he drills his narrative into the mind of his voters. He has chanted *"no Collusion"* 71 times on just Twitter.

He tried to make people believe him by telling them that collusion is not a crime. Hence everything the special counsel is doing is a witch hunt and out of a personal vendetta against him. Moreover, Trump and his allies have made this investigation questionable and tried to gain the support of the masses by projecting that the allegations are all fake. They have circulated the idea of the inquiry being a conspiracy of the *"deep state"* to demolish the democratic system and Trump's presidency. According to Trump, people are after him due to personal bias.

Some would think that the President of the Free State would be quite busy, but Trump has cried about a *"witch-hunt"* by tweeting it 183 times. That is not the only troublesome part. It is astonishing to know that according to a poll conducted by USA Today and Suffolk University, 50% of Americans believe in Trump's witch hunt complaints.

Legal experts hold a different view. Victoria Nourse, a professor at Georgetown Law, emailed USA Today: "Don't be fooled by word games. There is no legal term, for "Collusion." The legal term for collusion is the crime of conspiracy. If you agree to kill someone and take a step toward that (hired the killer, or encouraged the killer, met with the killer) you are guilty of conspiracy to commit murder."

She further added: "So, if you agree to defraud the US or disrupt the elections (even if it is not with the Russians) and you take a step forward (any step.... meetings, payments, etc.), that's a conspiracy."

Federal Conspiracy Statute 18 USC 371

The word collusion might not be a part of the legal documents, but President Trump's collusion can be called a political conspiracy — a conspiracy that required help from an enemy, a foreign state. The Federal conspiracy statute 18 USC 371 prohibits conspiracies that aim to defraud the United States. It states:

"If two or more persons conspire either to commit any offense against the United States or to defraud the United States, or any agency thereof in any manner or for any purpose, and one or more of such persons do any act to effect the object of the conspiracy, each shall be fined under this title or imprisoned not more than five years, or both. If, however, the offense, the commission of which is the object of the conspiracy, is a misdemeanor only, the punishment for such conspiracy shall not exceed the maximum punishment provided for such misdemeanor."

The code is quite clear about the conspiracy to commit an offense or defraud the US. Rudy Giuliani said: "The question is, 'What law, statute or rule or regulation's been violated?' Nobody has pointed to one." However, legal experts have answered Giuliani and argued that the meeting between Trump Jr. and the Russians at the Trump tower might have violated election laws that can be considered a conspiracy to defraud the government.

According to Stephen Schulhofer, a law professor at New York University, collusion can be classified into benign and criminal, depending on the situation. He agreed that planning or colluding with someone for any lawful purpose like arranging a game is benign collusion and not a crime. However, if a candidate running for candidacy colludes with the Russians and collaborates with them to meddle with the election process, then it is illegal and is certainly a crime.

13 Russians behind the Bars

In the light of the investigation conducted by Robert S. Mueller III, the special counsel, The U.S. Justice Department indicted 13 Russians and three companies on charges of running a complex network to influence the results of the 2016 election and assist in Trump's campaign. The network got its orders from St. Petersburg, Russia, and ran propaganda against Hillary Clinton on social media. They influenced American voters through online rumors and fake news and ultimately rallied the streets of election battleground states. These Russians were faking being American citizens and political activists. They built their campaign by playing on immigration, religion, and race cards to manipulate the election campaigns and made the elections more divisive.

These Russians were found to be in contact with some prominent names of the Trump campaign. These agents working under the Russian government's orders traveled across the United States and collected intelligence. This intelligence was then used strategically to cause political disruption and conflict. Their main targets were Colorado, Virginia, and Florida.

Mr. Mueller also found that 13 digital paid advertisements were circulated on social media. These were sponsored by Russians and targeted and trolled Mrs. Clinton and supported Mr. Trump.

The Popular Opinion

Even though Mueller's report did not explicitly accuse President Trump of colluding with President Putin of Russia, public opinion is already quite well established. Most Americans indeed felt optimistic about Trump after the report of the 22-month investigation did not directly accuse him of conspiracy and fraud.

However, the national opinion poll conducted has shown that the general public is still doubtful about the president's alleged ties to Russia. Public opinion did not fluctuate much even after U.S. Attorney General William Barr published his four-page summary of Mueller's investigation. Mr. Barr, in his brief, emphasized the point that Mueller found no evidence that the Trump campaign conspired with Russia in the 2016 election. Even though Trump called the summary *"complete and total exoneration,"* the public was not satisfied because the question regarding whether or not Trump obstructed the investigation remained unanswered. The poll asked Americans about their opinion on the allegations of collusion and obstruction of justice against President Trump. A whopping 48% believed, *"Trump or someone from his campaign worked with Russia to influence the 2016 election."*

Even more people, 53% to be exact, held the opinion that *"Trump tried to stop investigations into Russian influence on his administration."*

It was clear that political affiliations also greatly influenced public and representative opinions. More Democrats than Republicans believed that Trump colluded with Russia and obstructed justice.

In Plain Sight - Open Collusion

A recent statement by House Judiciary Committee chairman, Rep. Jerrold Nadler (D-N.Y.) declared that there was *"open collusion"* between President Trump's campaign and Russia. He believes that even if Robert Mueller did not find any substantial evidence to impeach and indict Trump, the collusion was explicit.

Nadler appeared on CBS' *"Face the Nation,"* where he explicitly said that Trump Jr. and Jared Kushner's 2016 meeting with the Russians at the Trump Tower was enough proof, and "there was in plain sight open collusion with the Russians." Mueller's report concluded the investigation without any definitive evidence of Trump's collusion with Russians or obstruction of justice.

That was followed by a four-page summary of the report submitted to Congress by Attorney General William Barr. Nadler was sure that no evidence was required to prove the collusion and obstruction since everything was apparent. He accused Barr of bias and said that for Barr, the interests of the White House came first.

When asked about his opposition to releasing the findings of the 1998 investigation by Special Prosecutor Kenneth Starr on former President Bill Clinton, Nadler answered by calling it a comparison between *apples and oranges.*

He remarked that he was against the release of the Starr report because it meant releasing grand jury information to the public rather than to Congress. Nadler remained neutral when asked to comment on whether the full Mueller report could have enough information to cause an impeachment.

He said, "there could be grounds for impeachment, there could be grounds for other actions, and there could be things the American people ought to know."

CHAPTER THREE

— • —

PART 1 DNI

I T TOOK MORE THAN just a vote to make America great again. The polls on the eve of the election had left everyone speechless. Many liberals questioned the sanity of the people in their states when Trump was elected as the President. A majority of the American population is rooted in Trump, but we still cannot rule out the possibility of foul play during this election.

The outrage at this election was not only confined to the US borders. There was an international cry of anger as citizens across the globe tried to imagine a new world with Trump as the President of the

United States. The man used to talk about bombing countries because they *"deserved"* to be bombed.

The fact is that no reason is good enough to annihilate people from different countries just because they assumed *"un-American."* The whites have always played the superhero whenever conflicts arise in the East. Their involvement revolves around their personal and national benefits above all else. They show the world a different face while hiding their true intentions behind the mask of selfishness. Voting for Trump as the President of the United States has proven the fact that hatred still runs in the veins of some modern Americans and their older generations. This free-world country is now slowly turning into a prison for legal immigrants. They seek refuge in a country that will never accept them; It is because of the many wars the US is waging across the world that causes the inflow of immigrants.

Many factors played a significant role in propelling Trump to the presidency.

The role played by the Director of National Intelligence (DNI) is crucial during Elections. The declassified reports of the DNI provide evidence of Putin's involvement during the 2016 US Elections. Putin has openly shared his opinions regarding Donald Trump and even claimed that he wanted Trump to become the President. To make this wish a reality, Russian President Vladimir Putin used his power to influence the campaign. He aided Donald Trump during the elections by undermining the public faith in the process held by the US Democrats. That would further denigrate Hillary Clinton, former secretary of state, to make it harder for her to win the elections.

The masses were not happy with either candidate running for President, but people always considered Clinton as an option between the lesser of two evils. As stated in previous chapters, a majority of Americans would have been enthusiastic regarding the Presidency if Bernie Sanders was still in play. Russian President Putin did everything in his power to harm Clinton's presidency and promote Pre-selected Trump. As expected, Donald J. Trump has denied the allegations of Putin's involvement openly. He had downplayed the claims presented by the right-wing media regarding Putin's participation during the electoral process. He has consistently denied being involved with Russian agents. The investigations regarding Russia's involvement will pursue for several months, but the former Trump administration official and a former campaign adviser had pleaded guilty to lying to federal agents about the communications that have taken place between them and the Russian nationals.

US Intelligence Agencies

High-ranking American Intelligence officials reported Putin's interference in the 2016 presidential election and favored Trump throughout the election period. The CIA and the FBI drafted and compiled this, along with the help of the National Security Agency.

This document blatantly stated that Putin had placed his orders to influence the campaign in the year of 2016 aimed at the presidential elections in the United States. The report noted that Putin sought to denigrate Secretary Clinton by showing a clear preference for President-elect Trump. The higher-ranking official of the agencies presented this report, which they later made public. By denying their claims, Trump was rejecting the importance and credibility of the Central Intelligence Agency. He kept a uniform stance against them and repeatedly told the public they made the reports up. On, one occasion, during one of his speeches against Mueller's investigation, he went on record to say that the CIA was on a 'witch hunt against him. Despite his several claims of a witch hunt, the witch hunt against Donald J. Trump continues despite his allegations of Russia's involvement being a 'hoax' and a 'scam.'

. His repeated demeanor holds the power to psychologically influence the masses by warping their view on the ongoing investigation. Deputy Attorney General Rod Rosenstein appointed Robert Muller to investigate and prove the collusion between Trump's campaign team and Russian officials in May 2017.

In February 2017, the Justice Department indicted thirteen Russian operatives and three companies on charges of waging information against the United States of America and interfering with the election to help Trump's campaign. A few days later, twelve Russian nationals were indicted on the counts of hacking the system of the Democratic National Committee, Hillary Clinton's presidential campaign. The intelligence agencies charged several of these hackers for working with the GRU agency, which is a part of Russia's military intelligence agency. Rod Rosenstein stated, *"The goal of the conspirators was to impact the election. What impact they may have had is a matter of speculation; that is not our responsibility."* He also includes *"no allegations of knowing involvement by anyone on the campaign and no allegations that the alleged hacking affected the election result."*

The Director of National Intelligence, Dan Coats, has warned his government colleagues against the danger posed by Russia regarding America's Cybersecurity. He has stated that the warning signs are present and the cyber system is blinking. As the Director of National Intelligence, he has presented a critical point while addressing the Hudson Institute of Washington DC in 2017. *"Today, the digital infrastructure that serves this country is literally under attack."*

Dan Coats has also claimed Russia is one of the most aggressive foreign factors for United States Intelligence. James Mattis, the Defense Secretary of the United States Intelligence, has backed up the findings of the US intelligence agencies tentatively. He has reaffirmed Russia's involvement during the 2016 presidential campaign. According to his statements, Russia had moderate to higher participation in influencing the elections in Trump's favor.

Propaganda Tools Used by Russia

There are many tools within our reach to influence the masses. Russia took advantage of several available tools to control the Presidential campaigns in Trump's favor. Social media has provided a platform for people to exercise their freedom of speech. The accessibility of social media can become dangerous as it holds the power to influence a majority of people psychologically, especially those who are highly active in these forums.

Russians created several fake accounts by having American names. These accounts then promoted Trump by creating slogans, campaigning on the internet, and then posting on public pages with high traffic. These accounts impersonated real Americans so that they could get the trust and attention of the average American citizen on a social forum. Owners of these accounts also paid for ads for promoting their posts, hence reaching the maximum amount of viewership. The Russians acted as an organization with several employees who ran these accounts to create political intensity by supporting radical groups to criticize Hillary Clinton. They neither criticized Trump, nor Bernie Sanders, nor did they speak in favor of these two individuals.

These accounts focused on various issues like immigration, terrorism, and freedom of speech; and approached sensitive topics like the Black Lives Matter movement with an astounding amount of blatant inconsideration. A Russian defendant, Irina Viktorovna Kaverzina, explained that she had created conflicting pictures and posts as an American. She had fooled the Americans who followed her to believe that their people wrote the post. Political rallies were promoted by such organizations through social media and were carried out in the country from June to November 2016. The page 'March for Trump' carried out following rallies and promoted them through social media pages.

ISIS and US – Mexico Borders

1. March for Trump carried out in New York on June 25, 2016

2. Support Hillary. Save American Muslims in Washington, DC on July 9, 2016.

3. Down with Hillary in New York on July 23, 2016.

4. Florida Goes Trump in several Florida cities on August 20, 2016.

5. Miners for Trump in several Pennsylvania cities on October 2, 2016.

6. Show your support for President-Elect Donald Trump in New York on November 12, 2016.

7. Trump is NOT my President in New York on November 12, 2016

8. Charlotte against Trump in Charlotte, NC. November 19, 2016.

There were many cases where the officials linked ISIS with the U.S.-Mexico borders. The entire campaign running for Donald Trump's presidency played with the hearts of Americans by invoking fear of the unknown. He invoked hatred with intolerant remarks in his speeches. Many people backed up Trump's allegations, including Jeff DeWitt. Donald Trump's state campaign chairman and Arizona State Treasurer maintained their stance on all public occasions no matter what Trump said.

Frequently, Trump has claimed that ISIS is coming over the border to attack American citizens. He has proclaimed that only one of the running presidential candidates can get rid of this *"problem"* and that is he, himself. Taking advantage of the *"make America Great Again"* slogan, he used hatred and fear to influence minds by involuntarily forcing them to vote for Trump.

Many other statements claimed the presence of ISIS in Mexico back in September 2014. No one could prove the claim to be right and no one, including a single law enforcement official, could confirm ISIS's presence within the city of Mexico. A right-leaning Judicial Watch cited a report from California Representative Duncan Hunter, who stated that Border Patrol agents caught ten ISIS fighters near the border of Texas back in October 2014.

However, the claim came out to be untrue when the Homeland Security spokeswoman of the US department, Marsha Catron, rebuked the claim as false. She noted that individual with ties to ISIS that were caught near the border is categorically incorrect and nothing more. He blamed immigration to be the root cause of the high rate of unemployment throughout the country.

Trump has given rise to patriotism on a whole different level and has continued to do so throughout his presidency period so far. He has blamed the immigrants–legal and illegal alike–for the atrocious crimes committed and reported in the news. He Tricks people to believe through a method of repeating his sentences have instilled fear of the unknown into the heart of those who support him.

Trump's thoughts on immigrants are as clear as day. Since the first date of his election campaign, he has openly shown his dislike for immigrants. Trump once asked the audience how to handle the migrants who are bringing crimes along with them. Someone shouted, *"Shoot them."* To everyone's surprise, the President laughed off the comment by making a joke out of it. *"Only in panhandle can you get away with such a statement."* The laid-back attitude of the President shows that he would be okay with any other Americans displaying similar behavior.

Trump has been playing with the blame game for long enough to fuel a wrong sense of patriotism inside people's hearts. He has blamed illegal immigrants by stating that they have hurt 'African-Americans' and 'Hispanic Americans' by taking minimum wage jobs from them. There was a hidden message behind such statements where he believed that minorities opt for minimum wage jobs on their own. By sparking hatred and debate regarding the immigrants who seek refuge in the United States, Trump has raised many eyebrows. These migrants contribute to the American way of life and work hard every day. However, thanks to Trump, their contributions are forgotten. They are remembered by many as 'drug dealers, criminals, and rapists.'

Several Mexican families are crossing the borders to reach America in despicable conditions, but it is not a topic of emergency for the President. These families put their lives and safety at risk even when migrating through legal means. They are entering a new stage of life and into a place where they know no one. No one would voluntarily put themselves at a disadvantage by moving to a country where they have no connections, to begin with. Such families only migrate to the United States to seek better life opportunities and healthcare facilities. The country of the United States of America may seem like a savior from afar, but they slowly learn the dark truth of unacceptance and discrimination that minorities often face as they slowly adjust to their new life.

Not All Immigrants Are Illegal

Most immigrants are legal and go through several screenings and background checks to make sure that the individual migrating into the country is not a criminal. However, illegal immigrants were not able to cross the borders since 2008. The country has enforced stronger border patrolling and has ceased the activity of unlawful crossing at the borders.

Undocumented immigration includes unlawful entry of foreign nationals into the country and staying back in the country after their entry visa or parole documents expire. Illegal immigration has been one of the most heated topics of debate since the 1980s. It has also been a focus of pre-elect and post-elect President Donald J. Trump. He was the one who promoted building a wall near the Mexico border to keep the immigrants out.

CHAPTER FOUR

PART 2 DNI

Trump has instilled the fear of Mexicans crossing the border and coming to kill all of them. As a result, tens of millions of Americans are now worried about so-called gangsters, rapists, and criminals coming to target them. So much so, the American government is ready to spend $5.7 billion on a border wall to stop Mexicans from coming in. That is all for what? Trump is only doing that because he tirelessly reinforced the theme that he will protect Americans from criminal immigrants.

The surprising thing is that the people who live not more than 350 miles away from the border are not in support of the wall Trump is building to bar Mexicans from stepping foot on American soil. In other words, the people who are supposedly living on the frontlines of what Trump calls a crisis zone are those who are least inclined to support the idea that Trump has proposed. Thousands of families, women, and children who try to cross the border and seek asylum in America are treated inappropriately.

That is why the Mexican border crisis is more of a humanitarian crisis. The United States border is not designed to deal with and take care of families and children. That is the role it has been forced to play. The results, of course, are tragic and disturbing.

According to Kevin McAleenan, Customs and Border Protection Commissioner, *"the infrastructure is not compatible with the reality of who is getting apprehended."* He essentially admitted that his agency is ill-equipped to take care of the people currently entering the US.

As shocking as it may seem, Border Patrol does not have the right standards for detention conditions.

There is a good reason why that is. Border Patrol is not supposed to detain people trying to cross the border for any meaningful amount of time. The problem arises when Border Patrol detains Mexicans for days, and sometimes for weeks.

Before the deaths of two children in December 2018, it had been a decade since an incident like this was reported. No child had died in the custody of Border Patrol in ten years. When Jakelin Caal Maquin died on December 8, 2018, it raised questions about how Border Patrol manages and deals with immigrants. Do they even get the medical attention that they need or not? Similarly, the death of the second child, Felipe Alonzo Gomez on Christmas Day provoked a separate set of questions.

Why a child was held in Border Patrol custody for six days before ICE was even asked to find a spot for him and his father, and why he was shuffled between four facilities, including being taken from the hospital to a cramped highway checkpoint?

It is time to face the truth. The Mexican border crisis is a humanitarian crisis, and constructing a wall cannot solve this crisis. The thing is that the point of building this high-price wall is to keep Mexicans from entering America undetected. The funny thing is that it is not what the Mexican families and children, trying to cross the border, are doing.

They are turning themselves into the nearest border agent and seeking asylum on the U.S. side. They want to enter America legally. That is something they have a legal right to do. The specific problem with the Trump administration is not that they are unable to catch the immigrants. The problem is that they cannot deport them soon enough. They can also not detain them for the entire time until they are deported. That is because of extra-legal protection needed to give to families and children. The Trump administration calls these laws *"loopholes"* in the system, which have created the policy of catch and release. To Trump, the policy of catch and release is a crisis because it leads to a large number of immigrants to release into the US.

There Is No Evidence of Terrorist Activity near the Border Area

Even before the election, during his campaign, Trump claimed claim that the US border is not safe because of all the Mexicans trying to enter America. He blatantly labeled Mexicans as *"terrorists"* who were all set to make America unsafe.

According to NBC, a total of only six known or suspected terrorists tried to cross the border, and that too was in the first six months of 2018. Other than that, no reported case would confirm the presence of Mexican terrorists in the border area. Moreover, there is no evidence that Mexicans are causing any unrest in the area alternatively if they are a threat to the locals of that area.

It seems like the Trump administration is adamant that Mexicans are all alien migrants who are potentially dangerous and should get screened additionally because of factors they might have in common with terrorists. Just because Trump considers a country to be hostile and friendly to terrorism does not mean America can ban the nationals of these countries. Sadly, that is what Trump has done.

Trump and his administration have repeatedly fed Americans lies and propaganda statements, about the US Army involvement in Syria, ISIS, and the Mexican border crisis. The more we look into these matters, the more we will identify the lies and misstatements that Trump made up to rouse the feelings of patriotism in Americans and steal their votes. Now that Trump has taken office, he would do anything in his power to prove the claims he made authentic and statistically correct.

CHAPTER FIVE

THE ATTORNEY FROM KREMLIN

ONCE CHOSEN AS THE Republican nominee for the presidency, Donald Trump's presidential campaign launched on June 16, 2015. Within one year, on June 2016, Trump's son Donald Jr., his son-in-law Jared Kushner, and then-campaign manager Paul Manafort were sitting in a well-organized meeting at the Trump Tower with Russians, who promised to "incriminate Hillary and her dealings with Russia." The meeting remained in the shadows until the investigation into the Russian collusion kicked in after the U.S. Elections of 2016.

The Infamous Email - Russia - Clinton - Private and Confidential

Rob Goldstone, a British Publicist, and music manager were undoubtedly unaware of the turn his life was about to take when he played the role of the fixer on June 3, 2016. The former tabloid reporter became a part of the biggest scandals of the U.S. elections when he contacted Donald Trump Jr. and offered to arrange a meeting with a Russian lawyer from the Kremlin, Natalia Veselnitskaya. Goldstone brokered the meeting over an email sent to Trump Jr., which he later forwarded to the senior members of the Trump campaign. The timing of the email was crucial since Donald J. Trump was about to start his hostile and controversial election campaign, which was aimed to destroy his opponent, Hillary Clinton's image.

The Trumps knew Goldstone back from the Miss Universe 2013 pageant which took place in Moscow and was co-owned by Donald Trump Sr.; the President's father and a famous business tycoon. It was during the same pageant that Trump tweeted Vladimir Putin and invited him to attend the pageant as well as a meeting. Although Putin canceled at the last minute, he sent an embellished lacquered box, a traditional Russian gift, and a note through Aras Agalarov.

Even though Trump Jr. described Rob as a mere 'acquaintance,' the email thread released by Goldstone made it clear that he was more than that. Goldstone was the manager for Emin Agalarov, an Azerbaijani pop singer and businessman, who also happened to be one of the performers at the beauty pageant. Emin is the son of an oligarch and prominent real estate developer in Moscow, Aras Agalarov. It was on the orders of Emin that Goldstone emailed Trump Jr. The Agalarovs also came into the circle of Mueller's inquiry when it hinted that a telephonic conversation took place between Trump Jr. and Emin Agalarov, something that both parties conveniently failed to recall. On the morning of June 3, 2016, Rob Goldstone wrote in his email:

"Emin just called and asked me to contact you with something very interesting.

The Crown prosecutor of Russia met with his father Aras this morning and in their meeting offered to provide the Trump campaign with some official documents and information that would incriminate Hillary and her dealings with Russia and would be very useful to your father.

This is very high-level and sensitive information but is part of Russia and its government's support for Mr. Trump—helped along by Aras and Emin.

What do you think is the best way to handle this information and would you be able to speak to Emin about it directly? I can also send this info to your father via Rhona, but it is ultra-sensitive so wanted to send it to you first."

It was clear from the email that Putin was a supporter of Trump and wanted him to win the elections. Trump received a helping hand from him through the offer of 'official documents' against Hillary Clinton. These documents were most probably the emails that were hacked by Russian hackers and leaked later on. The email quite explicitly told that this offer came directly from the government of Russia and was very important for Presidential Candidate Trump.

Upon receiving this email, Trump Jr. replied within a few minutes:

"Thanks, Rob. I appreciate that. I am on the road at the moment, but perhaps I just speak to Emin first. Seems we have some time and if it's what you say I love it, especially later in the summer. Could we do a call first thing next week when I am back?"

Goldstone sent a timely reply under the subject of 'Russia - Clinton - private and confidential and read: *"Let me know when you are free to talk with Emin by phone about this Hillary info — you had mentioned early this week so wanted to try to schedule a time and day."* Trump Jr. provided his cellphone number and showed a willingness to speak on a call.

Goldstone told him that since Emin Agalarov was on stage, he will call in about 20 minutes. Then Trump Jr. received a call from a blocked number and called Emin back afterward. The offer was accepted and after a few emails, the date and time of the meeting with the *"Crown Prosecutor of Russia"* were fixed to be held on June 9, 2016, at 4 pm at the Trump Tower.

It was decided that Goldstone would not sit throughout the meeting but will escort the Russians to 725 Fifth Ave, 25th floor, and introduce them. Trump Jr. forwarded the email thread to Jared Kushner and Paul Manafort, the two men who were going to be a part of the meeting.

About his role in the arrangement of the meeting and the entire email exchange, Goldstone told CNN that sending those emails was one of his regrets, and he was only helping his client arrange a meeting by collecting necessary information. In front of the Senate committee, Trump Jr. claimed that he could not recall the call from the blocked number. However, it is a well-known fact now that Donald Trump's Trump Tower residence number is a blocked one.

Participants of the Meeting

As promised, Goldstone brought and introduced the Russian party to Donald Trump Jr. and his confidants: Jared Kushner – President Trump's son-in-law and current senior adviser, and Paul Manafort. Trump's then-presidential campaign's chairman, former lawyer, and a convicted felon. Even though Goldstone did not want to attend the meeting, he stayed when requested by Trump Jr. That was done to have an equal number of participants on both sides.

The Russian attendees included Natalia Veselnitskaya, the attorney from the Kremlin who allegedly had the material that could tip the scales toward Trump and ruin Hillary's chances of winning the presidency. There were a translator, Anatoli Samochornov, and a businessman, Ike

Kaveladze, who had links with a Russian oligarch. Another key figure was Rinat Akhmetshin, a Russian lobbyist who was well-connected with Russian counterintelligence operations.

In the statement issued in July 2017, Natalia denied the allegations of working on orders from the Kremlin or producing any sensitive material against Clinton. Rinat Akhmetshin also clarified that his real intention was to discuss the Magnitsky Act and its amendment. Whereas, Ike Kaveladze, the businessman, maintained the stance that he was just a representative of the Agalarov family.

Trump Tower Meeting

Although the participants were the only people fully aware of what happened at the meeting, Trump Jr. described the details of the meeting to Hannity, and in doing so, he skipped the part where he had to tell about the things he learned. The meeting took place on June 9, 2016, at 4 pm at the Trump Tower, as planned.

Trump Jr. called the meeting *"sort of nonsensical, inane, and garbled."* Maybe the translator was not doing a good job. He said that the Russians went on and on about Russian adoption and requested help in that matter. He called the meeting downright dull, and due to this, Jared Kushner left within a few minutes, and Manafort was busy on his phone.

Mueller's Report also highlighted the fact that once Jared Kushner knew that the attorney had nothing exciting or big enough to undermine Clinton, he tried to get out of the meeting. He even emailed two of his assistants to call him so that he can leave with an excuse.

They followed orders, and Kushner was out of the meeting, a long time before it ended. Paul Manafort was noting down pointers on his phone during this time. These were the same notes that the Senate Judiciary Committee presented to him during the investigation. The records were a jumbled-up pile of different references and Veselnitskaya's memo. There was even a typing error or autocorrected line where instead of DNC, it read *"Active sponsors of RNC."* The memo also mentioned two individuals linked with Browder and called them *"the main sponsor of the Democrats."*

Veselnitskaya appeared in an interview on NBC as well and added her piece of information to the story and said that the only thing that Trump Jr. was interested in knowing was whether she had any financial records to prove that illegal sources sponsored Clinton's campaign. Trump Jr. accepted that it was the whole point of the meeting after all. He was disappointed that the pretext was like *'Hey, I have information about your opponent,'* whereas the reality was like *'Hey, some DNC donors may have done something, and Russia and they didn't pay taxes,'* this made Trump Jr. frustrated.

In another statement about the meeting, Trump Jr. described by saying: *"After pleasantries were exchanged, the woman stated that she had information that individuals connected to Russia were funding the Democratic National Committee and supporting Ms. Clinton.......... No details or supporting information was provided or even offered."*

When the meeting came to an end, Trump Jr. recalls that Goldstone came to him and apologized for wasting their time.

Lies and Conflicting Statements

The various statements regarding the nature and aim of the meeting and the contradictions in them were enough to spill the beans. At first, Trump Jr. fed the story of the meeting being *"primarily about adoptions"* to the press. Soon after, he changed his statement and referred to it as a *"short introductory meeting"* related to *"a program about the adoption of Russian children."* Not many days had passed before he finally accepted that the meeting was arranged and conducted to get any possible *'dirt'* on Clinton that the Russians can provide. He expected to receive some inside Intel that could help his father win.

Though according to him he did not get his hands on anything significant about the Democratic nominee, and the meeting was all about the Magnitsky Act, an American law that blacklists human rights abusers and because of which Putin has banned Americans from adopting Russian kids.

President Trump's 'wonderful' son said: *"I asked Jared and Paul to stop by. We primarily discussed a program about the adoption of Russian children that was active and popular with American families years ago and was since ended by the Russian government, but it was not a campaign issue at the time, and there was no follow-up."* He said that when the meeting was arranged, the Russian lawyer was *"vague, ambiguous, and made no sense"* about Clinton and that *"she had no meaningful information"* about her.

The lawyer of Trump Jr. issued a formal statement in which he said that Natalia Veselnitskaya hinted that she had private information about some people linked with Kremlin, who were sponsoring and backing Clinton's presidential campaign. However, she did not have anything substantial to prove her claims. In Trump Jr.'s opinion, the attorney's *"true agenda all along"* was to discuss the adoption issue, and she just used the pretext of political information to get the meeting arranged. In his own words, the meeting was *"nothing... a wasted 20 minutes"*. As soon as Trump Jr. learned that the New York Times was planning to leak his emails, he, himself, published his emails on social media via tweets. He did this to save his skin and prevent any further damage. In his tweets, he clarified that the emails were just *'political opposition research.*

Maybe he needed some law lessons to understand that gaining anything valuable from foreign governments to help win an election is considered illegal in America nonetheless. The Russian version was also quite flawed. The attorney who was called the 'Crowned attorney of Russia' told her side of the story. She said she wanted to inform Trump Jr. about a company that had committed tax evasion in Russia and funded the Democratic campaign.

She said the company was linked to William Browder, who was a donor as well as a supporter of the Magnitsky Act. During an interview, she reportedly said: *"I never had any damaging or sensitive information about Hillary Clinton. It was never my intention to have that."* What is even more alarming is how fast she changed her statements.

After denying all accusations of being related to the Russian government in any sense, she finally accepted that she was receiving her orders from the Russian Prosecutor General's office, namely from Prosecutor General Yury Chaika. She was asked to provide Trump Jr. with all the information regarding the Magnitsky Act, which she had collected during her investigation.

Rinat Akhmetshin presented another justification on July 14 during an interview. He said that the attorney claimed to have proof that someone, who was sponsoring the Democratic campaign had violated Russian law. He said that Veselnitskaya briefed Trump Jr. and provided a document regarding the same.

After the Meeting – Email Leaks

The entire timeline has the footsteps of collusion since the meeting on June 9, 2016, was followed by a report by The Washington Post, which revealed that the hackers might be Russian in origin. According to the Mueller Report, the email systems were breached in April, and soon after, a professor with ties to the Russian government told George Papadopoulos, an adviser to Trump's campaign, that Russians had found *'dirt'* on Hillary Clinton. A day before the meeting, Russian agents established a website named DCLeaks. As soon as the meeting concluded, Democratic National Committee (DNC) emails hacked by Russian intelligence hackers (as per Mueller's report) first leaked on DCLeaks, and soon WikiLeaks decided to publish them too on July 22, 2016. That was a strategically chosen move since the 2016 Democratic National Convention was held right after that. There were 19,252 emails with 8,034 attached files. The emails were exchanged between DNC members from January 2015 to May 2016.

Another batch of 8,263 emails followed the earlier leak, which was released in November of the same year.

Even though WikiLeaks denied any allegations of receiving emails from Russia, Special Counsel Robert Mueller announced that 12 Russian agents of a group called Fancy Bear conducted the cyber-attack. As per the investigation by the CIA, the US Intelligence Community believed that Russia was behind the leakage of the emails, and it was an attempt to sabotage Hillary Clinton's campaign. The agencies also claimed that Kremlin directly linked the providers of these emails to WikiLeaks.

In November 2016, the security agencies announced that that they were *"confident that the Russian Government directed the recent compromises of emails from US persons and institutions, including from US political organizations."*

A CNN news report on October 14, 2016, also announced that Julian Assange received the emails from the Russian government, and *"there is mounting evidence that the Russian government is supplying WikiLeaks with hacked emails about the US presidential election."* Another factor that substantiates the doubts about Julian Assange's plausible connection with the Russian collusion was WikiLeaks' avid interest in leaking the material exclusively on Ms. Clinton in 2016.

During the election campaign, WikiLeaks did not publish any other information and exposed no individual other than Hillary. The website continued to concentrate all its efforts to damage the reputation of the DNC and its nominee. What is even more surprising is that WikiLeaks outright refused to publish anything that was not related to the US election 2016. The leaks were timed to come out at the most crucial moments of Hillary's campaign. Not long after, in November 2017, Trump Jr. was accused of being in contact with WikiLeaks via Twitter during the election campaign. The conversation between the official

Twitter handles revealed that WikiLeaks was an active participant in the campaign and even provided services of an election advisor for President Trump. WikiLeaks suggested that Trump should cry foul play and refuse to accept the results if it seems he is about to lose.

Julian Assange also asked Trump Jr. to support his claim that Hillary Clinton devised to use drones on him. Moreover, a link to the website was also shared where the public could access the emails. WikiLeaks tried to claim its prize once Trump was elected as the president by requesting that Australia should be forced to appoint Julian Assange as ambassador to the US.

Trump's Defense

Donald Trump tweeted at 5:35 am on August 5, 2018:

"Fake News reporting, a complete fabrication, that I am concerned about the meeting my wonderful son, Donald, had in Trump Tower. That was a

meeting to get information on an opponent, totally legal and done all the time in politics - and it went nowhere. I did not know about it!" The Twitter ramblings by President Trump were nothing new, as he continued to call it all a witch hunt and fake news. He adamantly denied knowing anything about the meeting before it took place.

When the news about the meeting was out in the open in July 2017, President Trump maintained his stance while talking to the New York Times by saying: *"No, I didn't know anything about the meeting... must have been a very unimportant meeting, because I never even heard about it."*

He changed his statement slightly the second time he interacted with the press and said: *"I only heard about it two or three days ago."*

President's version was supported by his son when he came before the Senate Judiciary Committee on September 2017 to testify that he told his father nothing about the emails he had received or sent. When asked why he replied: *"because I wouldn't bring him anything that's unsubstantiated"* and *"because it had nothing to do with him."* Another matter in which the President got involved was Trump Jr.'s initial statement about the meeting. The statement described '*adoption*' as the prime reason for the meeting. That was misleading since that was surely not what Trump Jr. went looking for. The emails were clear proof. The Washington Post reported about a month later that the President was very much a part of the statement drafting process. In fact, he was involved to the extent that he dictated the statement word-for-word to his communications director, Hope Hicks, during a return flight from Europe. He was returning after his first meeting with Russian President, Vladimir Putin in July 2017.

Jay Sekulow, Trump's lawyer, called this news inconsequential, misinformed, inaccurate, and not pertinent. He said that Trump was not involved in drafting the statement. On July 12, 2017, Sekulow said, *"I was not involved in the statement drafting at all, nor was the President."*

This claim was proven to be a lie when the President's legal team submitted a letter to Meuller's investigation and admitted that Trump *"dictated a short but accurate response."* Even the letter was not entirely truthful because the statement was anything but accurate. It was a cover-up and failed to tell what had happened and how. According to the President, what his son did was completely legal. During a press conference on July 13, 2017, he defended his son and said:

"My son is a wonderful young man. He took a meeting with a Russian lawyer, not a government lawyer but a Russian lawyer ... I think, from a practical standpoint, most people would have taken that meeting. It's called opposition research, or even research into your opponent.

I've had many people —I have only been in politics for two years, but I've had many people call up — "Oh, gee, we have information on this factor or this person, or, frankly, Hillary." That's very standard in politics. Politics is not the nicest business in the world, but it's very standard where they have information, and you take the information."

Trump Knew All About It

Hillary Clinton's most retweeted tweet has to be the one in which she tagged Donald Trump and wrote: *Delete your account.* In replying to Clinton's tweet, Donald tweeted: How long did it take your staff of 823 people to think that up--and where are your 33,000 emails that you deleted? That might have seemed a great comeback, but if we connect the dots, it will become clear that this tweet about the emails came just 40 minutes after the Trump Tower Meeting was scheduled.

Even though the President and his team of attorneys and officials claimed that he had no idea about the meeting and only found out about it a few days ago, people read between the lines when Trump continued being a loudmouth on Twitter. Another teaser tweet by Trump came out on June 7, which further fanned doubts about Trump being informed about the meeting. In it, he said that he would give a *'major speech'* and would talk about *"all the things that have taken place with the Clintons."*

When he had grabbed the primaries from California, Montana, New Mexico, South Dakota, and New Jersey, he spoke to the audience and announced: *"I am going to give a major speech on probably Monday of next week, and we're going to be discussing all of the things that have taken place with the Clintons. I think you're going to find it very informative and very, very interesting. I wonder if the press will want to attend. Who knows?"* Although the speech was postponed to June 22, Trump was over-excited and had high hopes of getting dirt on his opponent during the upcoming meeting at that time. Michael Cohen, Trump's then-lawyer and fixer, publicly testified that Trump knew it all, and Don Jr. certainly informed his father about the meeting before it, though he did not mention Russia at that time. The former lawyer was present, and so were many others when the Russian meeting proposal was discussed and accepted. Cohen's claims have been reported in Mueller's report, but they cannot be proven because of the lack of substantial evidence.

Moreover, Steve Bannon, while talking to the journalist Michael Wolff said that there was 'zero' chance of Trump not being involved in the meeting. Another incident that caught the attention of the Democrats was the call Trump Jr. made to a blocked number between two conversations with Agalarov. Don Jr. may have said that he could not recall whom he spoke to, but Trump's residence also uses a blocked line.

Russian Attorney & Obstruction of Justice

The critical character of this scandal was Natalya Veselnitskaya, the 43-years-old Russian attorney who promised to provide sensitive information on Clinton. Even though collusion could not be proven, she got charged with the crimes of obstruction of justice, along with an unrelated civil money laundering and forfeiture case. She might save from facing charges for her secret meeting, but she was accused and indicted by a Federal court in New York City on another case. She filed an *"intentionally misleading"* document to save the corruption and money laundering of Russian government officials. She was on the FBI's *"wanted"* list.

At the Trump Tower meeting, she also discussed something associated with the scheme on which the civil case, U.S. vs. Prevezon Holdings, was based. It was a case of a $230 million tax refund fraud scheme, and she acted criminally as a lawyer. The case was filed in 2013 as an effort to recover property valued at millions of dollars in New York City. It was a method to launder large sums of money and evade tax.

Russian accountant named Sergei Magnitsky helped uncover the scheme and was taken into custody when he secretly reported the fraud to the Russian government. When Magnitsky died during his time behind bars, a U.S. law named the Magnitsky Act was passed in 2012. During the Trump Tower meeting, Veselnitskaya requested Trump's support against this act. Ironically, Natalia flew to the U.S. not to attend the meeting but to attend a court hearing for an appeal of the money laundering case.

CHAPTER SIX

— • —

SAME DAY CYBER-ATTACK ON DNC AFTER THEN CANDIDATE PRESIDENT TRUMP ASKS RUSSIA TO FIND MISSING EMAILS FROM HILLARY CLINTON

HILLARY CLINTON'S EMAILS GETTING exposed to the public was perhaps the most significant turning point in the United States Elections 2016. The leak came out of nowhere and swept the nation off its feet within a few hours. One can only imagine the amount of planning that went into it. As the news of these leaks took the country by storm, DNC officials began to allege that the Russian government was behind the breach. As expected, the reported hack that stole Hillary Clinton's presidency continued to cloud the proceedings of the 2016 elections from that point onwards.

Following the allegations made by the Democratic National Committee (DNC), United States Intelligence increasingly shared the same opinion. The doubt that the Russian government turned the tables on Hillary Clinton turned into a fact when several top cybersecurity researchers claimed that the allegations were indeed right.

A Brief History of the Notorious Hack

The news of the infamous hack of the Democratic National Committee first broke in mid-June, 2016. That was when Crowdstrike, a firm known for analyzing threats to network security revealed that the DNC had called it in to inspect the servers of the party and found two separate Russian intelligence-affiliated adversaries in the DNC network. As alarming as it sounds, Crowdstrike also revealed that one of the hacking groups had access to the DNC servers for almost a year. The same fact was later mentioned in the Director of National

Intelligence report – Russia had access to the DNC from July 2015 to June 2016.

A day after Crowdstrike released its report, someone calling himself Guccifer 2.0, which kind of implied his association with the notorious hacker Guccifer, claimed responsibility for the hack. He did that in a blog post. Through the blog post and an accompanying Twitter account, Guccifer 2.0 completely refuted the claims made by Crowdstrike that the hack was orchestrated by Russian intelligence. Instead, Guccifer 2.0 went on to call himself a *"lone hacker."* Moreover, he claimed to have handed much of the stolen information from the DNC networks to WikiLeaks. In the beginning, the authenticity of Guccifer 2.0 was taken into consideration. That led to Roger Stone, an American political consultant, author, lobbyist, and strategist known for his opposition research mostly for the candidates of the Republican Party, being dragged into the case.

For those who do not know, Roger Stone is known as a veteran of dark political arts and was a longtime advisor to Donald Trump, but he left the Trump campaign on August 8, 2015. When his part in the hack was investigated, two of his associates said that he collaborated with WikiLeaks founder, Julian Assange, during the 2016 presidential campaign to discredit and defame Hillary Clinton.

Both Stone and Assange denied these claims. However, the next week, two cybersecurity firms named Fidelis Cybersecurity, and Mandiant independently corroborated the initial assessment made by Crowdstrike that it was indeed Russian hackers who infiltrated the DNC networks. They also revealed to have found that the two groups that hacked into the DNC used malware and methods that were identical to those used in other attacks perpetrated by the same Russian hacking groups. The evidence against Russia did not end there. The most compelling piece of evidence, linking the DNC breach to Russia, was found by Thomas Rid, a professor at King's College in London, at the beginning of July. He unveiled an identical command-and-control address hardcoded into the DNC malware that was also discovered on malware used to hack the German Parliament in 2015. According to German security officials, it was Russian military intelligence malware.

The evidence just began to mount from there. There were numerous traces of metadata in the document dump that revealed various indications that proved the stolen documents translated into Cyrillic script – a writing system used for various alphabets across Eurasia, especially Eastern European countries, including Russia. Another proof that rendered the authenticity of Guccifer 2.0 was that he claimed to be from Romania. However, he was not able to chat with the Motherboard journalist in fluent Romanian. In light of all this evidence, it determined that this sort of hacking attempt could not have been carried out outside of Russian norms.

According to Morgan Marquis-Boire, a malware expert who works with CitizenLab, "It doesn't strain credulity to look to the Russians. That is not the first time that Russian hackers have been behind intrusions in the US government, and it seems unlikely that it will be the last."

The biggest reason to believe that the mastermind behind this hack was Russia was that the country has carried out similar intrusive hacks previously. In 2015, breached the White House and State Department email servers. They were able to glean information even from President Obama's Blackberry.

The Kremlin, of course, denied Russian involvement in the DNC breach.

Here's what Dmitry Peskov, the Kremlin's spokesman, told the Reuters news agency in Moscow, "I completely rule out a possibility that the [Russian] government or the government bodies have been involved in this."

Was Guccifer 2.0 a Lone Hacker?

As compelling as all the pieces of evidence are, there is still a shred of possibility that Guccifer 2.0 could have been an alone actor motivated by hacktivist principles of dismantling state power. After all, he would not be the first lone hacker to do so. In an interview that he gave with NBC, Julian Assange of WikiLeaks denied the claims that his whistleblowing organization works in collusion with Russian intelligence.

In the interview, Julian Assange said, *"Well, there is no proof of that whatsoever. We have not disclosed our source, and of course, this is a diversion that's being pushed by the Hillary Clinton campaign."*

On the other hand, it is hard to ignore that this is the same Julian Assange who is responsible for helping Snowden find a home in Russia. It is also hard to ignore that WikiLeaks publicly criticized the Panama Papers for exposing the financial misdeeds of Putin. Assange also frequently criticized Hillary Clinton's time at the State Department.

A massive leak the weekend before Clinton's nomination seems to align with both Russian interests and Assange's own. There is no denying the fact that the billionaire GOP candidate is a longtime admirer of Vladimir Putin. Putin too would prefer Trump's presidency because Trump made it very clear that he will not necessarily defend NATO allies against a Russian invasion.

On top of it all, Paul Manafort, Trump's campaign manager, formerly worked as an advisor to Viktor Yanukovych, the Russian-backed President of Ukraine before he was sent into exile in 2014.

According to Marquis-Boire, *"Due to the nature and timing of this hack, it all seems very political."* If truth be told, the timing of this hack was simply perfect and seemed carefully planned. The timing confirmed that it was a political move rather than the work of a lone hacker.

Trump's Urge to Search for Missing Emails

The controversy stirred by a likely Russian hack of the DNC had not quite settled down when Trump made it more evident that the hack was indeed carried out by Russian operatives. The GOP presidential candidate, at a press conference in Florida, responded to a reporter's question by urging Russia to do him a favor. He invited Russia to collect and leak the missing emails that were deleted from the private server Hillary Clinton used while she was the Secretary of State during the Obama administration.

Donald Trump publicly said, "Russia, if you're listening, I hope you're able to find the 30,000 emails that are missing. I think you'll be rewarded mightily by our press." He later came back to the same topic, telling the reporters, "If Russia or China or any other country has those emails, to be honest with you, I'd love to see them."

The Clinton campaign didn't waste much time and issued a timely statement, saying, "This has to be the first time that a major presidential candidate has actively encouraged a foreign power to conduct espionage against his political opponent. This has gone from being a matter of curiosity and a matter of politics to being a matter of national security."

That very same day, Russian spies initiated their attempts to hack Hillary Clinton's email server. Robert Mueller's indictment stated that the Russian hackers made their first attempt to break into Clinton's office email accounts after hours on July 27, 2016, to retrieve emails she had deleted because they were not related to government work.

It's worthy of notice that Trump's press conference started in the morning in Florida, and late afternoon in Russia. The very same day, the Russian hackers tried to access not only Clinton's email server but also 76 more email addresses of people active in the Clinton campaign. The prosecutors said the spies began hacking on July 27, 2016, but the indictment does not suggest a direct link with Trump's request.

The 29-page indictment filed by Robert Mueller tells the story of a cyber-attack of the highest order on the Democratic Party establishment, which was working to elect Hillary Clinton. The indictment mentioned that Russia also conspired to hack the computer systems of state elections authorities and election equipment manufacturers to steal sensitive and confidential information of American voters.

The indictment went on to reveal that an unidentified U.S. congressional candidate received stolen documents related to his or her opponent from the Russian hackers in August 2016. The Russian operatives also gave large amounts of defamatory data to a state-registered lobbyist and a reporter.

According to the indictment, the prosecutors found 12 Russian hackers, who were working for the GRU military intelligence agency, used spear phishing, a crude and conventional technique, to access the email accounts of useful victims, including Hillary Clinton's campaign chairman, John Podesta. Moreover, the hackers used Bitcoin and various fake American identities to build a computer infrastructure for the planned cyber-attacks. On March 19, 2016, Podesta got an email disguised as a security notification from Google, instructing him to change his password by clicking on the given link. As it turned out, that email was not from Google. It was from Aleksey Lukashev, a senior lieutenant in the Russian military. When Podesta clicked on the link, he innocently gave Russian intelligence complete access to his account.

According to Mueller, the hackers promptly stole more than 50,000 emails. According to the indictment, the hackers also created a fake email account that seemingly appeared to be from a Clinton campaign staffer. The said email account was used to email 30 other associates of Clinton, a spreadsheet on the candidate's poll ratings. Mueller stated that this link directed the recipients to a website created by the GRU.

In April 2016, the Russian operatives used a spear phish and installed spying software on the computer network of the Democratic Campaign

Committee (DCCC or D-triple-C). The spying software allowed the hackers to take screenshots of their monitors and record what employees were typing on their keyboards. As the Russian hackers were spying on the activity of DCCC workers, one of them also had access to the DNC. That is when the hackers gained access to 33 DNC computers. That is what Mueller reported. After gaining the much-desired access, the hackers allegedly searched for documents by using words, such as *"Trump"* and *"Hillary,"* and stole thousands of emails and confidential information on voter outreach, Democratic fundraising, and several other activities.

Mueller stated that gigabytes of data were funneled out of the DNC and DCCC by the hackers and sent to remote servers rented by the Russians in Illinois and Arizona. Lieutenant Captain Nikolay Kozachek and Second Lieutenant Artem Malyshev were allegedly caught when they were logging into the Arizona server to download their haul.

Once the stolen emails and information were dealt with, the hackers efficiently deleted files to cover their tracks and pushed their electronic loot on to unsuspicious American public. The hackers created various online personas, such as DCLeaks, which claimed to be a group of *"American hacktivists,"* and Guccifer 2.0, which claimed to be a lone Romanian hacker. From June 2016, these screen names operated their websites, along with Twitter and Facebook pages, to publish emails the hackers had stolen from the Democrats. According to the indictment, WikiLeaks joined the efforts in July. On July 6, Mueller said that WikiLeaks demanded the Russians give it all the damaging material about Clinton in time for the Democratic convention in Philadelphia. WikiLeaks allegedly wanted to ruin Hillary Clinton's efforts to unite the party after a confrontational primary with Bernie Sanders. WikiLeaks' wish was granted, and emails showing neutral party officials working to promote Clinton over Sanders soon leaked. That is when

Chairwoman Debbie Wasserman Schultz resigned, which threw the party convention into disarray.

From that point onward, the leaks kept on coming. On October 7, 2016, soon after the leaked recording in which Trump bragged about grabbing women by their genitals, WikiLeaks published all the emails stolen from John Podesta. Another 32 sets of 50,000 messages followed this leak in total over the following month. On January 7, 2017, U.S. Intelligence published a fantastic report, alleging that Russia carried out a successful influence campaign geared toward undermining the United States electoral process and helping Trump enter the White House. Within a week, Mueller's team noticed the Russian hackers published a statement on the blog site attributed to Guccifer 2.0, claiming the Russian government had nothing to do with the hacks and leaks. As history is the witness, eight days later, Donald Trump was inaugurated.

Roger Stone... Guilty or Not Guilty?

On July 3, 2018, Ellen Huvelle, U.S. District Court Judge dismissed a lawsuit filed by a political activist group called Protect Democracy. Alleging that the Trump campaign and Roger Stone conspired with Russia and WikiLeaks, referred to in the indictment as *"Organization 1"*, to publish the hacked DNC emails during the 2016 presidential election race. The lawsuit was dismissed because the judge found it brought in the wrong jurisdiction.

In the following week, two government officials identified Roger Stone as the anonymous person the Russian hackers, operating the online persona Guccifer 2.0 (a cover for Russian spies), communicated. That was the same anonymous person who was mentioned in Mueller's indictment released by Deputy Attorney General Rod Rosenstein and Russian military intelligence officials with conspiring to interfere in the 2016 United States elections.

On January 25, 2019, Stone was arrested at his Fort Lauderdale, Florida, residence in a pre-dawn raid. His arrest was in connection with Robert Mueller's Special Counsel Investigation. Stone was charged in the indictment with witness tampering, obstructing an official proceeding, and five counts of making false statements. He pleaded not guilty and said he would fight the charges as they were nothing but politically motivated. Later, however, Stone acknowledged messaging Guccifer 2.0.

The prosecutors alleged that following the first WikiLeaks release of the hacked DNC emails in July 2016, a senior Trump campaign official contacted Stone and asked for any additional releases. The unknown senior official also inquired if there was other damaging information WikiLeaks had about the Clinton campaign. The indictment alleged that Stone also informed the officials about possible future releases of damaging material by WikiLeaks.

As of May 2019, he is pending prosecution by the United States Attorney for the District of Columbia.

The result of the FBI's Investigation for Clinton's Use of Private Email

The FBI launched an investigation into Hillary Clinton's use of a private email server during her tenure as Secretary of State. That was the email server that she used for her regular correspondence. The investigators, after a thorough investigation, concluded that Hillary Clinton had been *"negligent"* and *"extremely careless."* However, no evidence of a successful intrusion from an outside party was found.

FBI director, James Comey, stated, *"We did not find direct evidence that it was hacked successfully but given the nature of the system and the actors involved we would be unlikely to see such activity."* Although the FBI did not recommend charges against Clinton, the director stated that some of her emails might have been hacked. He said, *"Although we did not find definitive proof of this, it is possible that hostile actors gained access."* Comey went on to say *that the private email accounts of some of the people Clinton had been in contact with had been hacked."*

"Although we did not find clear evidence that the secretary or colleagues intended to violate laws, there is evidence that they were extremely careless in their handling of highly classified information," Comey said.

The FBI finally lifted the looming threat of criminal charges against Hillary Clinton, but James Comey's remarks clouded the chances of Clinton's electoral victory. He said there was evidence to support the FBI's verdict and that any reasonable person should have known that an unclassified server was no place for that kind of information.

"None of these [classified] emails should have been on any kind of unclassified server." The FBI director pointed out.

At the end of the year-long investigation in the light of laws designed to protect classified government data, Hillary Clinton was ultimately held responsible for whatever harm came from the leaked emails. The FBI revealed that 30,000 emails were returned to the state department. One hundred ten emails in a total of 52 chains contained classified information at the time they were sent. Eight of those email chains contained top-secret information, 36 chains contained secret information, and eight chains contained confidential information.

On the other hand, surprisingly, Clinton always insisted that she did not send or receive classified emails using her private email account. After the completion of the investigation, Obama came out in support of Clinton and argued at length that she is the *"steadiest"* and the most responsible choice for president.

Here is what Obama said, *"Hillary Clinton has been tested. She has seen up close what's involved. She's seen the consequences of things working well and things not working well. There has never been any man or woman more qualified for this office than Hillary Clinton. Ever. And that's the truth. That's the truth."* Come to think of it, there's nothing new.

Russia has always been considered a formidable foe in cyberspace. However, in the past five years, there has been a thousand-fold increase in its espionage campaign against the West. They always feel under siege.

Following the Western sanctions that were imposed on Russia after the country successfully annexed Crimea in Ukraine, the Russian economy got severely disrupted and hurt. Those sanctions led the Russian government to focus on increasing its theft of intellectual property in order to limit the impact of import restrictions. If we keep Russia's growing isolation in perspective, we would realize that the country has an increased need for intelligence, which the government fulfills by perpetrating highly sophisticated cyber-attacks. Due to the intelligence gathered as a direct result of these cyber-attacks, the Russian government can understand, manipulate, and influence political decisions in other countries.

CHAPTER SEVEN

— · —

MANAFORT AND YANUKOVYCH

I T'S ALMOST IMPOSSIBLE NOT to be aware of the legal proceedings of Paul Manafort's trials. His name has been all over the news in the last few years. For those who don't follow politics and current affairs, Paul Manafort is an American lobbyist, former lawyer, political consultant, and on top of it all, a convicted felon.

Manafort has served as a longtime Republican Party campaign consultant. To refresh your memory, Manafort joined the current American president, Donald Trump's presidential campaign team back in March 2016. He stayed as Trump's campaign chairman from June to August 2016. Following that, in 2018, he was convicted of bank and tax fraud.

Paul Manafort is not a new name to surface out of nowhere. The man has served as an advisor to the American presidential campaigns of GOP candidates, including Gerald Ford, Ronald Reagan, George H. W. Bush, and Bob Dole. However, Manafort's achievements do not end there. He has lobbied on behalf of several foreign leaders such as former Ukrainian president Viktor Yanukovych, the former dictator of the Philippines Ferdinand Marcos, the former dictator of Zaire Mobutu Sese Seko, and Angolan guerilla leader Jonas Savimbi.

Paul Manafort and His Secret Ledger

On one of the leafy side streets off Independence Square in Kyiv, there is an office that is known to be used for years by Donald Trump's campaign chairman. That was when he served as an advisor to Ukraine's ruling political party. The office in question is preserved in its original condition with all of Manafort's furniture and personal items.

While Manafort was in the capital of the United States, Ukrainian government investigators thoroughly examined some secret records and found his name. It wasn't just his name that popped up in the investigation. His links with the companies he sought business with were also exposed. The mission of this investigation was to untangle a corrupt network that was allegedly used to loot Ukrainian assets. And to influence the elections during the administration of Mr. Manafort's key client, the former president of Ukraine, Viktor F. Yanukovych. Among the evidence that the investigators gathered, there were handwritten ledgers that showed $12.7 million in undisclosed cash payments designated for Manafort from the pro-Russian political party of Yanukovych from 2007 to 2012. The figure quoted above is, according to Ukraine's newly formed National Anti-Corruption Bureau. Investigators asserted that the disbursements were part of an illegal book system, and its recipients also included other election officials.

In addition to all of that, criminal prosecutors in Ukraine also investigated a group of offshore shell companies. That helped people from Yanukovych's inner circle finance their extravagant lifestyles, including a palatial presidential residence that comprises a private golf course, zoo, and tennis court. Among the hundreds of shady transactions. These companies were engaged in an $18 million deal. To sell Ukrainian cable television assets to a partnership firm formed by Manafort and a Russian oligarch, Oleg Deripaska, who is known to be a close ally of Russian President Vladimir Putin.

Manafort and His Murky Involvements

It was not that Paul Manafort's involvement with moneyed assets in Ukraine and Russia came to everyone's attention for the first time. His participation in all the illegal activities had come to light previously. Still, now they became a pressing issue in the presidential campaign. And it led Manafort to resign from the designation of Trump's presidential campaign chairman just after five days these reports surfaced.

Owing to Trump's favorable statements about Putin and his annexation of Crimea and the suspected Russian hacking of Democrat's emails, Manafort's involvement in all these activities was taken far more seriously than ever before. His actions were examined more carefully, and new details of how he mixed business and politics came to everyone's attention. How Manafort benefitted from powerful interests is also currently under scrutiny by the new government formed in Kyiv.

Ukrainian anti-corruption officials said that the payments for Manafort, which were previously unreported, were a prime focus of their investigation. However, they did not have any substantial evidence on whether Manafort received those payments or not. Manafort was not a target in the separate inquiry into offshore activities, but the prosecutors stated he must have realized the implications of his financial dealings.

According to Vitaliy Kasko, a former senior official with the general prosecutor's office in Kyiv, "Manafort understood what was happening in Ukraine. It would have to be clear to any reasonable person that the Yanukovych clan when it came to power, was engaged in corruption. It's impossible to imagine a person would look at this and think, 'Everything is all right.'"

During the investigation, Manafort chose not to respond to the payment-related interview questions directed at him. However, his lawyer, Richard A. Hibey, said Manafort did not receive any such cash payments blatantly described by the anti-corruption officials. Hibey also disputed Kasko's suggestion that Manafort countenanced corruption or was involved with people who were engaged in illegal activities.

"These are suspicions, and probably heavily politically tinged ones. It is difficult to respect any kind of allegation of the sort being made here to smear

someone when there is no proof, and we deny there ever could be such proof," said Mr. Hibey.

Covert Payments

The rapid developments in Ukraine bring out the risky nature of international consulting, which was the basis of Manafort's business since the 1980s. That was the time when he went to work for the Philippine dictator, Ferdinand Marcos. Before Manafort joined Trump's campaign, his most prominent client was Yanukovych, who deposed in an infamous uprising, just like Marcos.

Before Yanukovych fled to Russia in 2014, he and his Party of Regions used to heavily rely on the advice given by Manafort and his firm, who helped the party win several elections. During that time, Manafort did not register as a foreign agent with the United States Justice Department. It is a requirement for those who wish to influence American policy on behalf of their external clients.

Nevertheless, it is not clear whether or not Manafort's activities required registering. If his services were limited to advising the Party of Regions in Ukraine only, he probably didn't have to register. However, Manafort also worked on polishing his client's image in the West. And he assisted Yanukovych's administration in drafting a detailed report, thereby defending the prosecution of Yulia V. Tymoshenko, his chief rival in 2012. Manafort lacked registration with the department which requires disclosing the amount the registrant paid and by whom the compensations he received from his foreign clients have remained covert and mysterious. However, a cache of documents discovered after the fall of Yanukovych's government has provided some answers.

The papers, commonly referred to as the black ledger in Ukraine, are nothing but scribbled Cyrillic that covers almost 400 pages. These papers took from the books that were once stored in a room located on the third floor of the former Party of

Regions headquarters on Lipskaya Street in Kyiv. The said room contained two safes stuffed with $100 bills, according to Taras V. Chornovil, a former party leader who was also a recipient of the money on several occasions. The man said in an interview that he had once received $10,000 for a trip to Europe.

Chornovil said, "This was our cash. They had it on the table, stacks of money, and they had lists of who to pay."

According to Chornovil, he left the party in part over rising concerns about the book's activity.

The National Anti-Corruption Bureau, which obtained the ledger, said in a statement, "Mr. Manafort's name appears 22 times in the documents over five years, with payments totaling $12.7 million. The purpose of the payments is not clear. Nor is the outcome, since the handwritten entries cannot be cross-referenced against banking records, and the signatures for receipt have not yet been verified."

The bureau went on to say, "Paul Manafort is among those names on the list of so-called 'black accounts of the Party of Regions,' which the detectives of the National Anti-Corruption Bureau of Ukraine are investigating. We emphasize that the presence of P. Manafort's name in the list does not mean that he got the money because the signatures that appear in the column of recipients could belong to other people."

The accounting records surfaced in the year 2016 when Serhiy A. Leshchenko, a member of the Ukrainian parliament who told he had received a partial copy from an unidentified source, published line items covering six months of outlays in 2012 totaling $66 million.

In an interview, Leshchenko said, "Another source had provided the entire multiyear ledger to Viktor M. Trepak, a former deputy director of the domestic intelligence agency of Ukraine, the S.B.U., who passed it to the National Anti-Corruption Bureau."

It is important to note that the bureau's funding is mandated under American and European Union aid programs, and it also has evidence sharing agreement with the FBI. Thus, it has investigatory powers, but it cannot indict suspects. Only if it passes its findings to prosecutors, which didn't happen in the case of Manafort, does the subject of its inquiry become part of a criminal case?

In the black ledger, individual disbursements are ranging from a few hundred dollars to millions of dollars. In the records from the year 2012, there is one payment of $67,000 for a watch, and another of $8.4 million made to the owner of an advertising agency for running the GOP campaign before elections that year.

According to Daria N. Kaleniuk, the executive director of the Anti-Corruption Action Center in Kyiv, "It's a very vivid example of how political parties are financed in Ukraine. It represents the very dirty cash economy in Ukraine."

Manafort's Involvement with Offshore Companies

For as long as Manafort worked in Ukraine, he also positioned himself to profit from corporate deals that benefited from the connections he had gained through his political consulting. According to the court filings, one of the arrangements which Manafort was part of involved a network of offshore companies. Which as per the report of government investigators, was used to launder public assets and money supposedly stolen by cronies of the government.

The said network of companies comprised of shell companies whose actual owners were protected by the secrecy laws; that prevailed in the offshore jurisdictions where these companies were registered. These countries included the British Virgin Islands, Seychelles, and Belize.

In an interview, Serhiy V. Gorbatyuk, Ukraine's special prosecutor for high-level corruption cases pointed to an open file on his desk. That contained paperwork for one of the shell companies called Milltown Corporate Services Ltd. This company played a vital role in the state's purchase of two oil derricks for $785 million. In other words, these derricks were claimed to be worth twice their actual amounts.

"This," Serhiy said, "was an offshore company used often by Yanukovych's entourage."

The role that the offshore companies played in business dealings involving Paul Manafort came to light owing to court filings in the Cayman Islands and a federal court in Virginia. These filings were related to an investment fund, Pericles Emerging Markets. Manafort and several other partners started the fund back in 2007. And its major supporter was Oleg Deripaska, the Russian mogul who was denied a visa by the State Department apparently because of allegations that linked him to Russian organized crime. A charge repeatedly denied by Deripaska.

Deripaska agreed to give $100 million to Pericles so the fund could afford assets in Ukraine and other countries in Eastern Europe. These assets included Black Sea Cable, a regional cable television and communications company. However, corporate records and court filings proved that it was barely a straightforward transaction.

Deripaska later stated that he invested $18.9 million in Pericles back in 2008 to complete the acquisition of Black Sea Cable. However, the said acquisition of the Black Sea assets has since become a point of contention between Deripaska and Manafort. In 2014, Deripaska filed a lawsuit in a Cayman Islands court in an attempt to recover his investment in Pericles. He also claimed he had paid about $7.3 million worth of management fees to the fund over two years.

On the other hand, Manafort's lawyer, Hibey, disputed the Black Sea Cable deal contained in Deripaska's Cayman filings. Hibey said Deripaska had overseen details of the final transaction of the acquisition and denied that Manafort had received any management fees from Pericles. However, he said that Rick Gates, one of Manafort's partners, who was also working on the Trump campaign, had received a small sum.

Manafort continued to work in Ukraine even after the downfall of Yanukovych's government. And to keep on helping allies of the exiled president to form a political bloc that opposed the new pro-Western administration. The Ukrainian company records gave no sign that Manafort formally dissolved the local branch of his company, Davis Manafort International. It was managed by his longtime assistant, Konstantin V. Kilimnik.

The Trials of Manafort

The numerous indictments filed against Paul Manafort were divided into two trials.

1. *Eastern District of Virginia*

In the Eastern District of Virginia, Manafort was investigated on 18 charges, including bank fraud, tax evasion, and hiding foreign bank accounts. The financial crimes of Manafort were uncovered in the United States during the special counsel's investigation into Russia's suspicious role in the

2016 election. The trial began on July 31, 2018, and on August 21, the jury presented its verdict.

The jury found Manafort guilty on 8 of the 18 charges. The remaining ten counts were declared a mistrial. Manafort was convicted on five counts of tax fraud, one of the four counts of failing to disclose his foreign bank accounts, and two counts of bank fraud. Mueller's office advised the court that Manafort should receive a sentence of 20 to 24 years, which is in line with federal guidelines. However, on March 7, 2019, the court sentenced Manafort to just 47 months in prison, less than nine months for the time already served. The court stated that the sentence recommended by Mueller's office was excessive and that Manafort had lived a blameless life.

2. District of Columbia

Manafort's trial in the United States District Court for the District of Columbia was scheduled on September 2018. He was charged with conspiracy to deceive the United States, not registering as a foreign lobbyist, money laundering, making false statements to investigators, and witness tampering. On September 14, 2018, Manafort daringly entered into a plea deal with prosecutors and pleaded guilty to two charges – witness tampering, and conspiracy to defraud the United States. Moreover, he agreed to forfeit more than $22 million in cash and property to the government and to cooperate with the Special Counsel fully.

On November 26, 2018, Mueller's office stated that Manafort had repeatedly lied to prosecutors about several matters and breached the terms of his plea agreement. Manafort's attorneys disputed the statement. On December 7, 2018, Mueller's office filed a document with the court that listed five areas in which according to them, Manafort lied and breached the terms he agreed upon in the plea agreement. DC District Court judge ruled on February 13, 2019, that Manafort had violated his plea deal by openly lying to the prosecutors.

In a hearing that took place on February 7, 2019, the prosecutors stated that Manafort concealed facts about his wrongdoings to increase the possibility of receiving a pardon. They speculated that Manafort continued to work in Ukraine after he had made his plea deal. Consequently, on March 13, 2019, the judge sentenced Manafort to 73 months in prison despite Manafort's apologies for his actions. 30 out of 73 months were concurrent with the jail time he received in the Virginia case.

Manafort was initially held at the United States Penitentiary Canaan in Waymart, Pennsylvania. As of now, he is held at, where he's referred to as inmate #35207-016. His expected release date is Dec. 25, 2024.

CHAPTER EIGHT

— · —

WIKILEAKS AND HILLARY CLINTON

I F THERE IS ONE question about the 2016 United States elections, that baffles the mind. It is, how did Hillary Clinton blow a 7 percent lead over Donald Trump, and that too in the final month of the campaign? The post-election analysis revolved mostly around FBI director James Comey's letter.

That he wrote to Congress, and less attention was paid to the role that WikiLeaks played until the news broke that the CIA blamed Russia for actively trying to help Trump win. The U.S. government stated that the Russian government allegedly hacked Hillary Clinton's campaign chairman John Podesta's emails. Those emails then made their way to WikiLeaks.

How Did WikiLeaks Affect the Election?

The hacked emails were published in series weekly during the entire month of October that year, so one was able to assess the effect these emails had on the campaign precisely. Also, many significant events took place during the final weeks of the campaign – the Comey letter, the debates, the Access Hollywood tape, etc. However, two things were assumed from the whole email fiasco. Americans were interested in the WikiLeaks releases, and the timeline of Clinton's downfall in the polls roughly matches the publishing schedule of the emails.

At first, Americans were paying too much attention to the WikiLeaks releases, even though all sorts of craziness was happening during those final weeks. Over 72 percent of people who searched for WikiLeaks from June onward also searched for the leaks during October or the first week of November as well. That piece of information is according to a report issued by Google Trends. A useful tool provided a rough estimate of what people, rather than the press, were focusing on.

The public's interest increased when Julian Assange announced in his press conference on October 4 that more information about the election would soon make it to WikiLeaks. About 40 percent of searches involving Trump and Clinton were initiated between October and the first week of November. Clinton's drop in the polls doesn't perfectly correlate with the spike in public interest in WikiLeaks. The day when WikiLeaks experienced the most searches in early October, Clinton's poll numbers were still rising. They continued to go up for another two weeks. There isn't one pivotal point that proves WikiLeaks caused Clinton's poll numbers to drop. The race was tightening before Comey sent his letter to Congress in late October. That was the time when Clinton's lead over Trump exceeded by seven percentage points.

When Comey released his letter, Clinton's lead went down to 5.7 percentage points. It's easy to conclude that Clinton's numbers would have risen further in early October had it not been for WikiLeaks. In that case, Trump would've had to fight off both the release of the Access Hollywood tape and lousy debate performances. The WikiLeaks emails made it clear that Clinton would be compromised if luckily, she became the president. As expected, the percentage of people who found Clinton to be trustworthy and honest stayed around 30 percent in polling throughout October and early November. The proof that WikiLeaks affected Clinton's chances of becoming the president is circumstantial.

According to National Exit Polls, Trump got to win among voters who decided to vote in October. That was Trump's best period to take over the election. Also, he won votes in the final week owing to Comey's letter, which had a significant impact on the ballot. It affected Clinton's lead rather severely, and the drop accelerated slightly afterward.

It wasn't just one thing that sank Clinton's ship. According to the evidence gathered, WikiLeaks is one of the factors that affected the presidential race and contributed to her loss.

The Extensive FBI Investigation

The highly sought-after emails released by WikiLeaks that created ripples in the American political landscape talked about various things. Lots of secrets were exposed, and many faces were unmasked in those emails. The anti-secrecy website, WikiLeaks, released tens of thousands of emails between the day these emails get unauthorized access and the day of the election. John Podesta, Clinton's campaign chairman, made an open claim that the Russian government was behind this mischief. He said Trump's campaign colluded with the Russian government and was well aware of what was going to happen. Needless to mention, Podesta was among the people whose emails were exposed to hackers. He refused to deny or confirm the authenticity of those emails, meaning some of those emails could have been doctored.

What followed the leak of Podesta's emails was the unraveling of the fact that Hillary Clinton broke government rules. By operating a private server from her upstate New York home while serving as the Secretary of State. According to the investigation led by the FBI, the dump of leaked emails inherently disclosed the following secrets:

Clinton Has Terrible Instincts!

On the same day that news of Clinton's private server broke, John Podesta emailed Neera Tanden, who worked for the Clinton campaign in 2008 and had remained a close advisor since then, to complain about Clinton's instincts.

"We've taken on a lot of water that won't be easy to pump out of the boat", Podesta wrote in September

2015 as Clinton's staff was afraid that Vice President Joe Biden would join the Democratic primary race.

"Most of that has to do with terrible decisions made pre-campaign, but a lot has to do with her instincts," Podesta had said in the email, to which Mrs. Tanden responded, "Almost no one knows better [than] me that her instincts can be terrible."

In the same email exchange, Podesta went on complaining that David Kendall, Clinton's lawyer, and Cheryl Mills and Philippe Reines, former State Department staffers, were not forthcoming with the facts.

Mrs. Tanden responded, "Why didn't they get this stuff out like 18 months ago? So crazy." Then she answered her own question by saying, "I guess I know the answer. They wanted to get away with it."

Following the leak of this email, Trump didn't take long to tweet the following message:

"If my people said the things about me that Podesta and Hillary's people said about her, I would fire them out of self-respect. "Bad instincts!"

Obama Lied Not Knowing about Clinton's Private Email Server

When President Obama said in an interview that he heard about Hillary's private email server at the 'same time everybody else learned it, through news reports,' the Clinton campaign exchanged emails within the group to say that the president was, in fact, not telling the truth.

The evening after Obama's interview aired, Clinton's spokesman Josh Schwerin emailed and said, "It looks like POTUS just said he found out HRC was using her personal email when he saw it in the news."

Clinton's former chief of staff, Cheryl Mills, responded, "We need to clean this up. He has emails from her – they do not say state.gov."

Mills' response implied Obama was undoubtedly aware that Clinton had a habit of using a private email server instead of the email account issued to her by the United States Department of State.

White House spokesman, Josh Earnest, rushed to the rescue to no avail and clarified that the president sure did exchange emails with Clinton, but he "was not aware of the details of how that email address and that server had been set up."

Morocco's "Quid Pro Quo"

The world identifies Hillary Clinton's aide Huma Abedin for her courageous and unwavering loyalty. However, she ended up tarnishing that reputation when she bluntly criticized her boss over a Clinton Foundation summit in Morocco.

In May 2015, at the time of the meeting in Marrakesh, Clinton was no longer serving as Secretary of State. However, she was about to announce her campaign for president during the event. Before the summit took place, Huma Abedin voiced her concern for four months and wanted to pull out. She warned in one of the emails leaked,

"If HRC was not part of it, the meeting was a non-starter. She created this mess, and she knows it."

This leaked email heavily implied that a $12 million donation from the king of Morocco was dependent on Hillary Clinton being there and attending the summit.

Huma Abedin wrote in her November 2014 email to campaign manager Robbie Mook, "Her presence was a condition for the Moroccans to proceed so there is no going back on this."

In the end, Hillary Clinton decided not to attend the summit and sent her husband Bill, and daughter Chelsea instead. As far as those $12 million are concerned, there is no record that the donation was received.

When the email leaked, Robbie Mook took the matter into his hands and tried to deal with the situation that had gone worse. By saying that there was no evidence of wrongdoing or *"quid pro quo."* He said that his exchange of emails with Huma Abedin did not show any scheduling distractions for Hillary Clinton.

Podesta Called Sanders "Doofus"...

In December 2015, John Podesta verbally attacked Hillary Clinton's primary election rival Bernie Sanders for giving inappropriate remarks and criticizing the Paris climate change agreement. Here's what Podesta wrote in one of the covert leaked emails:

"Can you believe that doofus Bernie attacked it?"

Later, Podesta was interviewed on CNN about it, and he admitted that he wrote the email in a state of severe frustration. He further said that his email did not affect his excellent relationship with the Vermont senator.

The Secret Syrian Action

That was perhaps one of the most secret emails that got leaked and stirred controversy. According to this email, Hillary Clinton told a Goldman Sachs conference that she would like to intervene in Syria secretly. She made this highly controversial remark in response to a question put up by Llyod Blankfein,

Goldman Sachs' chief executive, in 2013, months after she left office as secretary of state.

"My view was you intervene as covertly as possible for Americans to intervene." Hillary Clinton said to the employees of the bank in South Carolina. It acknowledged that the bank had paid her about $225,000 to give a speech.

That comment she made in the conference earned Clinton the reputation of being a war hawk by liberal critics. She went on to add "We used to be much better at this than we are now. Now, you know, everybody can't help themselves. They have to go out and tell their friendly reporters and somebody else: Look what we're doing, and I want credit for it."

A Warning to China

The leaked emails made Hillary Clinton come across as a warmonger. In one of the emails, Clinton had explicitly warned Chinese officials that if they were not willing or were not in the position to control North Korea's aggression, then the United States would be left with no other option but to put up missile defenses in the region.

"So, China, come on. You either control them, or we're going to have to defend against them." Clinton purportedly said at a Goldman Sachs conference in June 2013.

She also added that the United States would send additional warships to the region to counter the North Korean missile threat.

When Hillary Clinton was serving as the Secretary of State, she visited China seven times and helped develop Washington's *"pivot"* to Asia, a development that has long been viewed with suspicion by Beijing.

Attack on Catholicism

In 2011, an exchange of emails took place between Hillary Clinton's White House Director of Communications and a liberal think tank fellow John Halpin. Together they mocked a magazine article about media mogul Rupert Murdoch raising his kids as Catholics.

Halpin in one of the emails took the liberty of describing Catholics in his own words by saying, "Most powerful elements of the conservative movement are Catholics... they must be attracted to the systematic thought and [severely] backward gender relations." He further added, "It's an amazing bastardization of the faith".

Palmieri responded to that email and said those people must think *"it is the most socially acceptable politically conservative religion".* Later, Palmieri made a statement that she was also a Catholic.

Needy Latinos and 1 Easy Call

That was the subject line of an email sent by John Podesta to Hillary Clinton and her closest aide Huma Abedin in August 2015.

The email suggests Clinton reached out to former New Mexico Governor Bill Richardson and former Energy Secretary Federico Pena and asked for their help and support during her primary campaign. Podesta had also used a profane term to refer to Gov.

Richardson, who had implied in an email sent earlier that he would require a phone call to provide his support.

Clinton Campaign Was Fed a Question

According to one of the leaked emails, the former CNN contributor Donna Brazile notified the Clinton campaign in advance of a question Hillary Clinton would be asked at an event hosted by the cable network.

Donna Brazile wrote "From time to time I get the questions in advance" in the subject line of an email to Clinton aides. In the same email, Brazile pasted the text of a question pertaining to the death penalty that Clinton would be asked.

When WikiLeaks broke the news that Clinton was fed a question before the event, Brazile wrote in her statement: "I never had access to questions and would never have shared them with the candidates if I did."

The leaked email caused embarrassment for CNN as well, which Donald Trump later mockingly referred to as the *"Clinton News Network."*

When Brazile was serving as DNC vice-chair in January 2016, she forwarded to Clinton's staff an email that revealed the Sanders campaign's plan to court African-American voters. In response, Hillary's campaign spokesperson, Adrienne Elrod, responded, "Thank you for the heads up on this, Donna."

The fundamental objection raised by this email was that DNC was supposed to be neutral in the contest between Hillary Clinton and her Democratic primary season challenger, Bernie Sanders; however, it wasn't.

Justice Department Collusion

In 2015, Hillary Clinton's spokesman Brian Fallon wrote in an email, "DOJ folks inform me there is a status hearing, in this case, this morning."

Fallon was referring to a Freedom of Information Act request by a journalist and was trying to seek disclosure of Clinton's emails that she sent during her time as the secretary of state. Fallon is a former Department of Justice spokesman, and he was asking for information that was already made public. It was available and reported by multiple news outlets.

Still, Donald Trump criticized the communication between the Clinton campaign and the DOJ, saying, "This is collusion and corruption of the highest order."

Clinton Cautious of Refugees

Hillary Clinton made a paid speech in 2013 to the Jewish United Fund of Metropolitan Chicago, in which she said, *"Jordan and Turkey can't possibly vet all those refugees, so they don't know if jihadists are coming in along with legitimate refugees."*

Trump and his supporters seized on that remark to criticize Hillary Clinton for calling the United States to accept 65,000 refugees every year, which was way more than President Obama's plan to allow 10,000 every year.

Dreaming of Open Borders

Hillary Clinton's opposition to trade deals didn't quite match the remarks she made in a 2013 paid speech to the Brazilian bank Banco Itau. Clinton said, *"My dream is a hemispheric common market, with open trade and open borders, at some time in the future with energy that is as green and sustainable as we can get it, powering growth and opportunity for every person in the hemisphere."*

Critics highlighted that remark of Clinton and pointed to what Trump had been saying for months, *"Without a border, we just don't have a country".*

Hillary Clinton reportedly earned over $26 million for speeches that she gave after leaving the State Department.

The emails released on WikiLeaks acted as a deterrent. There's no denying the fact that people who were previously backing Hillary Clinton became concerned and doubtful of her intentions. The Trump campaign did not leave any stone unturned when it came to discredit Hillary

Clinton's ideas and speech remarks. The Trump campaign did everything in its power to add fuel to the fire as well as raise suspicion in the minds of people regarding Hillary Clinton's endeavors.

Chapter Nine

— · —

WikiLeaks, Julian Assange, and Russia

Does Russia benefit when WikiLeaks owner, Julian Assange, reveals the West's Secrets? This question has become more of a debate in the last few years, especially after the 2016 US election. According to American officials, Julian Assange and WikiLeaks don't probably seem to have any direct connections with Russian intelligence services. But it appears that WikiLeaks and Kremlin have the same agendas. How much of it is accurate and how much of it is not, or is somewhat open to interpretation?

Julian Assange was in one of his classic didactic forms when he was holding forth on the theme that consumes – the betrayal of big government and especially that of the United States. Assange, as the editor of WikiLeaks, rose to global fame back in the year 2010. It was when he released huge caches of highly confidential and classified American government documents that exposed the best secrets about its involvement in the Afghanistan and Iraq Wars.

The documents revealed the cynical diplomatic maneuvering of the American government all over the world as well. Since then, Julian Assange started to portray America as super-bully. He put forward the image of America as a nation that seems to have achieved imperial power by declaring allegiance to principles of human rights.

On the other hand, something that is missing from Assange's analysis is the criticism of another world power that is Russia, or its president, Vladimir V. Putin. Putin's government has not also lived up to WikiLeaks' standard of transparency. Putin's government has treated its opposition harshly by spying, jailing, sometimes assassinating opponents, and gaining control over the news media and the internet.

At the time of the 2016 US election, Assange and WikiLeaks were back in the spotlight, shaking the geopolitical scenario with new disclosures and a promise for coming up with more.

In July of that year, WikiLeaks released almost 20,000 Democratic National Committee emails. The release was suggesting that the party had conspired with Hillary Clinton's campaign to supersede her primary opponent, Senator Bernie Sanders. During those weeks, Assange expressed himself as openly critical of Hillary Clinton and promised the nation more leaks. That would upend her entire campaign against the Republican candidate, Donald J. Trump. American officials said that they were affirmative and had a high degree of confidence that the Russian government hacked the Democratic Party material.

They asserted the idea that the codes may have been stolen by the Russians also. That raised the question: Has WikiLeaks become a laundering machine for the material gathered by Russian spies? And more importantly, what is the precise nature of the relationship between Julian Assange and the Kremlin?

These questions became the center of discussion when American officials announced Russia played an essential role in the US presidential election campaign. Putin, who repeatedly clashed with Clinton when she was Secretary of State, publicly praised Trump, who blatantly returned the compliment. Trump even expressed his interest in developing closer ties with Russia and spoke favorably of Putin's annexation of Crimea. When WikiLeaks rose to prominence; Assange noted, saying he was motivated by a desire to use *"cryptography to protect human rights."* And that he would target authoritarian governments like Russia's.

However, the reality turned out to be the polar opposite of what he had said. A New York Times investigation of WikiLeaks' activities during the years Assange spent in exile revealed a different pattern. Whether by convenience, conviction, or coincidence, the documents released on WikiLeaks, along with all the statements that Assange gave. Russia seems to benefit at the expense of the West.

The emerging consensus among US officials is that Assange and WikiLeaks have no apparent ties to Russian intelligence. But in the case of Democrats' emails, Moscow knew it had a sympathetic ally in WikiLeaks where intermediaries would drop stolen documents in the anonymous digital inbox of the group.

Julian Assange was open about his views on America in an interview where he said, "Clinton and the Democrats are whipping up a neo-McCarthyist hysteria about Russia."

Assange made it clear there was no solid proof that what WikiLeaks releases comes from intelligence agencies. However, he said he would happily accept such material. In the same interview, Assange stated WikiLeaks was not created to serve a particular nation. It does not target nor spares any specific country. Instead, WikiLeaks works to verify whatever content it proffered in the service of the public. And it loves when it gets to show people a glimpse into the corrupt machinery that is in a constant attempt to rule them.

When Assange was asked about his policy for Russia and Kremlin, he described Russia as a bit of a player on the world stage when compared to countries like the United States and China. He said, "In any event, Kremlin corruption is an old story. Every man and his dog criticize Russia. It's a bit boring, isn't it?"

Since its inception, WikiLeaks has proved itself to be spectacular in some figures, like uncovering corruption, indiscriminate killing, and hypocrisy. Hence, many stand up and speak in favor of Assange and WikiLeaks, for instance, Gavin MacFadyen, who runs the Center for Investigative Journalism at the University of London. According to him, for Assange, the question is not where the information is coming from. What truly matters to him is if the material is accurate and in the public interest.

MacFadyen emphasized the worth of WikiLeaks by reminding us that intelligence services all over the world have a long history of using news organizations to plant stories.

There are people in the world that think Assange assumes an increasingly conservative approach. According to Andrei A. Soldatov, an investigative journalist who has written so much about Russia's security services, "The battle for transparency was supposed to be global; at least Assange claimed that at the beginning. Strangely this principle is not being applied to Assange himself and his dealings with one particular country, and that is Russia. He seems to think that one may compromise a lot fighting a bigger evil."

Support from Moscow

WikiLeaks was establishing its business in 2006 when Assange, who is an Australian national, sent a mission statement to potential collaborators. In that mission statement, he mentioned his ultimate goal was to expose the illegal or immoral behavior of governments in the West. Assange said it clearly that his main focus was the highly oppressive regimes in Russia, Eurasia, and China.

Shortly after WikiLeaks released the war logs in 2010, Assange lived up to his promise. He even told a Moscow newspaper that WikiLeaks had obtained compromising materials about Russia and its government and people in the business. However, Assange's life soon turned upside down. An international warrant was issued for his arrest when he got involved in allegations of sexual assault in Sweden. Of course, he denied the charges. Eight days later, WikiLeaks released a cache of State Department cables, which shed light on America's diplomatic relationships.

Assange himself pointed out in an interview that those cables involved rather blunt judgments on Russia. In one of the messages, Russia is referred to as a *"mafia state."* Those documents proved far more harmful to the United States' interests than to Russia's. The leak hardly affected Moscow. Russia's foreign minister, Sergey V. Lavrov, called Assange a "petty thief running around on the internet."

Later, Assange was asked in an interview if he still had the plan to expose the Kremlin's secret dealings. He replied, "Yes, indeed." However, that promise never materialized. Instead, as Assange's legal troubles began to mount, Putin decided to come to his defense.

When Hillary Clinton announced an investigation of WikiLeaks and vowed to take aggressive steps to deal with those responsible, Assange was arrested by the London police only to be interrogated by the Swedes. He came out on bail and held up in a Georgian country house from where he fought extradition. The house belonged to Vaughan Smith, who believed Assange was a victim of an "intense online bullying and disinformation campaign."

After only one day of Assange's arrest, Putin appeared at a news conference along with the French prime minister. He brushed off a journalist who suggested that the diplomatic cables released on WikiLeaks portrayed Russia as a communist nation and used the opportunity to bash the West.

"As far as democracy goes, it should be a complete democracy. Why then did they put Mr. Assange behind bars?" Putin asked. *"There's an American saying: He who lives in a glass house shouldn't throw stones."*

That wasn't the only time Putin came out in Assange's defense. He did the same several other times as well. He called the charges against Assange *"politically motivated"* and announced that the founder of WikiLeaks was being *"persecuted for spreading the information he received from the U.S. military regarding the actions of the US in the Middle East, including Iraq."*

As time progressed, Russia began to come out in full support of Assange. In January 2011, the Kremlin issued a visa for Assange, and one Russian was cited saying that Julian Assange is worthy of winning the Nobel Peace Prize. In April 2012, when WikiLeaks' funding began to dry up, and under American pressure. MasterCard and Visa stopped accepting donations, and Russia Today started to broadcast a show called *"The World Tomorrow"* with Julian Assange as its host. The amount of money Assange or WikiLeaks obtained for the 12 episodes remains unknown to this date.

However, Sunshine Press, which worked as Assange's spokesman, said in a written statement that Russia Today was not the only broadcaster that purchased the license to air the show. There were at least a dozen more broadcasters that purchased the license. On June 19, 2012, Assange's narrative took a different turn. He lost an appeal against extradition to Sweden and broke bail. He was granted asylum in a cramped embassy of Ecuador in London.

Assange's Plans for Moving to Russia

One year later, a man called Edward Snowden eclipsed Assange in terms of whistle-blowing fame. He was a National Security Agency contractor and is now a fugitive. He stunned the world and stressed out American alliances by leaking documents and revealing a US-led network of global surveillance programs. Snowden didn't give his thousands of confidential documents to WikiLeaks. However, Assange suggested that the flight he boarded in June of 2013 was bound for Moscow. That's where Snowden lives to this date after America canceled his passport.

"Now I thought, and advised Edward Snowden, that he would be safest in Moscow," Mr. Assange told the news program Democracy Now.

Years earlier, in a meeting with the New York Times in 2010, Assange expressed his interest in relocating to Russia and setting up WikiLeaks there. He was anticipating the likely fallout from the cables' release at the time. However, his associates were skeptical of the idea, considering the Kremlin's strict surveillance and tight control over the media.

It said that during his time in the isolated embassy of Ecuador in London, under constant surveillance, Assange's inherent mistrust of the West solidified. That's when he became numb to the abuses of the Kremlin and viewed them as a *"bulwark against Western imperialism,"* says one anonymous supporter.

Another person who worked for WikiLeaks in the past said, "Assange views everything through the prism of how he's treated. America and Hillary Clinton have caused him trouble, and Russia never has."

Daniel Domscheit-Berg, one of Assange's closest partners who quit WikiLeaks in 2010, said, "The result has been a "one-dimensional confrontation with the US."

It is easy to note that the biggest beneficiary of the confrontation, which played out in a series of public statements by Assange timed releases through WikiLeaks has mostly been Russia and Putin.

Assange at times has mildly criticized the Putin government. One such instance can be found in a 2011 interview, where he spoke of the *"Putinization"* of Russia. Then on Twitter, he also called attention to Pussy Riot, the punk band whose members insulted Putin, who was jailed. However, there are only a handful of instances where Assange criticized Russia or Putin. Mostly, he has remained silent about some of Putin's harshest moves. For example, it was Snowden, not Assange, who took to Twitter to condemn a law that gave the Kremlin extensive new surveillance powers. When Assange was questioned during an interview about his views on this new law, he acknowledged that

"Russia had undergone creeping authoritarianism." However, he suggested that *"that same development had occurred in the United States as well."*

Assange's Viewpoint on the Syrian Crisis

Besides all of that, Assange has also decidedly taken a pro-Russian view of conflict and hostilities in Ukraine, where the Obama administration accused Putin of favoring and supporting the separatists.

Sunshine Press, known to the world as the group's public relations voice, directed attention to the fact that in 2012 WikiLeaks also published an archive. It was called the Syria files, and it consisted of more than 2 million emails to and from the government of President Bashar al-Assad; whom Russia is brazenly supporting in Syria's ongoing civil war. At the time of the release, Assange's associate, Sarah Harrison, described the material as *"embarrassing to Syria, but it is also embarrassing to Syria's opponents."*

Since then, Assange has openly accused the United States of intentionally, consciously, and deliberately destabilizing the condition in Syria. The critical thing to note here is that Assange has not publicly criticized human rights abuses done by Bashar al-Assad and Russian forces fighting there.

The Panama Papers

In April 2016, the International Consortium of Investigative Journalists released a torrent of articles that reverberated around the world. By comprised of 11.5 million leaked documents from a Panamanian law firm that specializes in creating secretive offshore companies. The *"Panama Papers"* offered a look inside a shadowy world in which law firms, banks, and asset management companies help the world's rich and powerful people hide their wealth and avoid taxes.

The Panama Papers were the largest archive of leaked confidential documents that journalists had ever dealt with, so it didn't surprise anyone that in the beginning WikiLeaks was linked to the consortium's work on Twitter. However, what came as a shock to the journalists was what WikiLeaks did next.

Among the most significant stories exposed in the Panama Papers was one that showed how billions of dollars had wound up in shell companies controlled by a close friend of Putin's, Sergei P. Roldugin, a cellist by profession. More than a dozen news organizations, including two of Russia's last few independent newspapers, Novaya Gazeta and Vedomosti, also tried to trace the money.

However, WikiLeaks focused on just one thing – the Organized Crime and Corruption Reporting Project. WikiLeaks, in a series of tweets, after Roldugin was exposed publicly, thus questioned the reliability of the reporting. It highlighted that the said project had accepted grants from the Soros Foundation and the United States Agency for International Development.

In an interview with Al Jazeera, Assange reiterated the idea that the consortium had cherry-picked the documents to release, and that the Panama Papers were a pro-Western agenda. He said, "There was clearly a conscious effort to go with the Putin bashing, North Korea bashing, sanctions bashing, etc."

Putin saw WikiLeaks' stance on the controversy as an opportunity and defended himself. He declared that while the leaked documents suggest that "there is this friend of the Russian president, and they say he has done something, probably corruption-related there is no corruption involved at all. Besides, we now know from WikiLeaks that officials and state agencies in the United States are behind all this."

The consortium's director, Gerard Ryle, labeled Assange's statements as professional jealousy. The anonymous person who leaked the papers said in a manifesto that the Panama Papers first appeared to WikiLeaks. He confessed that multiple attempts were made to contact the organization, but none of them were answered. Assange claimed he did not know of that at all.

Andrei Soldatov, a Russian journalist, said in an interview that it was striking to see Snowden, who stuck in Moscow, is far more willing to criticize Putin than is Assange. Roman Shleynov, who collaborated on the project at Vedomosti and worked as an editor at the Organized Crime and Reporting Project, said that he too was *"at a loss"* and unable to explain Assange's attack on the Panama Papers.

"For me, it was a surprise that Assange was repeating the same excuse that our officials, even back in Soviet days, used to say — that it's all some conspiracy from abroad," Shleynov said. *"I understand his struggle with the United States, but I never thought he'd use our work, the work of Russian journalists, to make such a statement. I respected and still respect what Julian Assange has done, but I have changed my opinion of him as a person."*

Assange has repeatedly said, "I am WikiLeaks," and it seemed truer back then than ever. In an interview with The Times, Assange criticized the Panama Papers consortium for not releasing all the documents in its possession. He went on to call this act censorship. He said, "It is not the WikiLeaks model. It is the anti-WikiLeaks model."

In February 2016, Assange finally received legal news that he had hoped would change the game. The United Nations Working Group on Arbitrary

Detention ruled that he was being detained unreasonably and should release with compensation for the violation of his rights. However, the opinion was nonbinding and not accepted by Swedish and British courts.

What came next was a possible breakthrough. Swedish prosecutors agreed to question Assange about the rape allegations, but according to Melinda Taylor, one of Assange's lawyers, even if the Swedes refused to prosecute, Assange feared being held in Britain on bail-jumping charges. He was afraid he might be turned over to America, where an investigation into his activities remained open.

"The uncertainty gets to him," Taylor commented.

However, it seems what lifts Assange's spirit is publishing new leaks, like the Democrats' files. The work genuinely keeps him going.

CHAPTER TEN

KUSHNER MEETINGS

IT'S TIME TO SHIFT the narrative to Jared Kushner. For those who don't know, Kushner is Donald Trump's son-in-law and senior advisor. Mostly, he stays in the news for his alleged association with the Russians during the U.S. 2016 election and transition, which Kushner has denied repeatedly.

He released a statement to the Hill intelligence committees about his contacts with Russians during the presidential campaign, saying that he never colluded with the Russian government. According to Kushner, the Russian government was busy interfering in the election on its own and was determined to help the Trump campaign beat Democratic nominee Hillary Clinton.

A Peek into Kushner's Reputation

Jared Kushner was sworn in as Trump's senior advisor just days after the inauguration. He now leads a team to overhaul the federal bureaucracy by using private sector methods to bring the promises made by Trump's administration to fruition.

In May of 2017, news broke that the FBI was looking into Kushner as part of their ongoing Russia investigation. According to NBC, *"Investigators believe Kushner has significant information relevant to their inquiry, officials said. That does not mean they suspect him of a crime or intend to charge him."*

The FBI investigation was underway when the Washington Post reported that Kushner wanted to establish a secret communications channel with the Kremlin during Trump's transition period. Of course, this was being done with the consent of the US government.

"On July 24, Kushner testified in front of the Senate Intelligence Committee in a closed-door meeting regarding Russian interference in the 2016 election and Kushner's communication with Russian contacts during the campaign. In a statement following the meeting, Kushner said, "All of my actions were proper and occurred in the normal course of events of a very unique campaign."

In his prepared remarks, Kushner denied all the accusations of collusion. He said, *"I did not collude with Russians, nor do I know of anyone in the campaign who did. I had no improper contacts. I did not collude, nor know of anyone else in the campaign who colluded, with any foreign government."* Besides focusing on economic initiatives, Kushner also engaged in working with Secretary of State Rex Tillerson and Defense Secretary James Mattis on issues of national security and foreign policy. On the contrary, the Washington Post called Kushner out by saying he has no government or foreign policy experience. He is a shadow diplomat.

In November 2016, Trump said in an interview with the New York Times that his son-in-law "can help bring peace to the Middle East, despite the fact that Kushner has no foreign policy experience."

There is no denying the fact that Jared Kushner has been a favorite of his father-in-law. Why wouldn't he be? He is married to his beloved older daughter, Ivanka. Despite knowing that Kushner has no experience in government or politics, Trump came to rely on pieces of advice given to him by Kushner during the campaign. He said at a rally, *"Honestly, Jared is a very successful real estate person, but I actually think he likes politics more than he likes real estate. But he's very good at politics."*

Trump credited Kushner for masterminding the campaign's social media operation. Along with Trump's older children Donald Jr., Eric, and Ivanka, Kushner persuaded Trump to fire former Trump campaign manager Corey Lewandowski and to hire Reince Priebus as chief of staff. Furthermore, Kushner is known to have played a pivotal role in smoothing Trump's relationships with the GOP establishment, the American Israel Public Affairs Committee, and Fox News because he is friends with Rupert Murdoch, who owns Fox.

Kushner's Meeting with Kislyak

Kushner and Trump's first National Security Advisor, Michael Flynn, met with the then-Russian ambassador to the US, Sergey Kislyak, in the Trump Tower. There's a possibility that the meeting was about creating a secret back-channel communication between the Kremlin and the White House by using Russian diplomatic facilities.

According to U.S. officials' intelligence reports, this was planned to shield their pre-inauguration discussions from monitoring. Ambassador Kislyak informed his superiors in Moscow that Kushner proposed a meeting on Dec. 1 or 2 at Trump Tower. According to intercepted Russian communications reviewed by U.S. officials, Kislyak said Kushner suggested using Russian diplomatic facilities in the United States for the connections. Reportedly, Kislyak was taken aback by the idea of allowing Kushner to use Russian communications gear at its embassy because this proposal carried security risks for Moscow and the Trump team as well.

Russia sometimes feeds false information into communication streams that are monitored. This way, Russia sows misinformation and confusion among American analysts. However, it's not clear what Kislyak would have gained by falsely characterizing his contacts with Kushner in Moscow, especially when the Kremlin was hoping to improve relations with Trump dramatically.

Kushner's interest in establishing a secret channel with the Kremlin, instead of relying on American government systems added to the intrigue around the Trump administration's relations with Russia.

The U.S. intelligence officials said that even though Russian diplomats have secure means of communicating with Moscow. However, Kushner's request for access to such channels was unbelievable.

According to one former senior intelligence official, *"How would he trust that the Russians wouldn't leak it on their side?" The FBI would know that a Trump transition official was going in and out of the embassy, which would cause a great deal of concern. The entire idea seems extremely naive or absolutely crazy."*

The discussion of a secret channel is a testament to the fact that Trump's advisers were trying to hide their contact with the Russians. Everyone knows for a fact that Flynn was forced to resign after a series of false statements about his conversations with Kislyak surfaced. Also, Attorney General Jeff Sessions recused himself from matters about the Russia investigation once it was revealed that he remained silent and did not disclose his meetings with Kislyak when asked during congressional testimony if he had any contact with the Russians. It is common for senior advisers of a newly elected US president to be in contact with foreign officials and leaders. However, new administrations are always cautious when it comes to handling their interactions with Russia. Trump's administration had a strong reason to practice caution because U.S. intelligence agencies had accused Moscow of interfering in the presidential race and scheming to elect Trump. Russia, on the other hand, also would've had reasons to reject such an overture from Kushner. Had Kislyak said yes to Kushner's demands, it would've exposed Moscow's most sophisticated communications capabilities to Americans.

The Post received the first alert in mid-December by an anonymous letter, which said Kushner and Kislyak had talked about setting up a secret communications channel. The officials who reviewed the letter said the portion about establishing the secret channel was consistent with their understanding of events. For instance, according to the letter and those officials, Kushner told the Russians that he was aware it was politically inappropriate for them to meet publicly.

However, it was imperative for the Trump team to be in a position to continue communication with Russian government officials. In the same anonymous letter, it was mentioned that Kushner, Flynn, and Kislyak also talked about arranging a meeting between a Russian contact and a representative of Trump in a third unidentified country. The Post reported that Erik Prince, the founder of the private security firm Blackwater, now known as Academi, and an informal adviser to the Trump transition team, met a representative of Vladimir Putin on January 11, 2017 – 9 days before Trump's inauguration — in the Seychelles islands in the Indian Ocean. (According to Washington Post)

Michael Flynn on Friday, December 1, 2017, to lying to the F.B.I. regarding his previous contacts with the Russian ambassador, Kislyak. Though Mueller indicted Flynn for his contacts with Russia during the transition, Flynn's history of foreign ties long predates Trump's presidential run.

It is no longer a secret that just a few months before Flynn began advising Donald Trump on his presidential campaign, he was paid *"approximately forty thousand dollars"* to talk at an RT gala, where he was in the presence of Vladimir Putin, and his chief of staff, Sergei Ivanov. It stated that Julian Assange appeared at the celebration via videotape. Reportedly, Flynn accepted a hefty sum of money from other Russian companies also, including $11,250 for a speaking engagement for Kaspersky Lab, a Russian cybersecurity company with alleged ties to the Kremlin.

Kushner's Meeting with Gorkov

At Kislyak's request, Kushner met with Sergei Gorkov, the chief executive of VEB (Vnesheconombank), a Russian state-owned bank currently under U.S. sanctions. According to the reports, Kushner and Gorkov met for just under half an hour not long after Trump took office. Later on, that meeting was scrutinized by both Congress and the Justice Department, as part of their investigations into Trump's campaign which was allegedly influenced by Russian interference.

According to written testimony presented to the Senate Intelligence Committee, the head of the Russian state investment bank VEB presented Kushner with a gift: art, along with a bag of dirt from Kushner's ancestral village in the former Russian imperial territory of Belarus.

The White House and VEB have different versions of what happened in the meeting. In the testimony, Kushner said he had attended the meeting because he was informed Gorkov was a direct line to Putin and could give valuable insight into how the Russian President was viewing the new administration. According to Kushner, it was the best way to work together, and those specific policies were not discussed.

On the other hand, VEB described the meeting as essential to its developmental strategy. The bank was hit with American economic sanctions as a result of the role Russia played in the 2014 Ukraine crisis and its annexation of Crimea. Of course, the bank wanted those sanctions lifted. As of today, it remains unclear as to what was discussed in those 20-25 minutes, the timeframe Kushner gave later that day.

Sergey Kislyak arranged the meeting, but it's not clear why Russia chose to send Gorkov. A Moscow-based investor, who has pitched Gorkov on several occasions, said, *"Gorkov likes to do things differently. He's pretty rare in that sense. Maybe he was sent as an experiment to try a new approach with the Americans."*

Different people had different theories as to why Gorkov was the chosen one. According to Pavel Vrublevsky, the founder of Russian online payments firm ChronoPay, which shares business interests with VEB, *"It was obvious why the Russian government sent Gorkov to the States. It had to be someone with no oligarch status. Someone innovative."* Whatever may be the motive behind sending Gorkov to meet and win over Trump's son-in-law, did not work. According to Kushner's testimony, at the end of the meeting, the two said their goodbyes, and he has had no reason to connect with him since. Also, the sanctions imposed on VEB were never lifted.

Kushner Pressed for the Dismissal of Comey as FBI Director

The Wall Street Journal reported that Jared Kushner insisted on firing James Comey as FBI director. Trump listened to his senior advisor and acted as advised. Special Counsel Robert Mueller investigated the firing as a possible attempt to obstruct truth and justice.

The Wall Street Journal cited different reasons as to why Kushner would push Trump to remove Comey as FBI director. According to one source, the dismissal of Comey would be supported by displeased FBI agents who thought Comey did not handle Hillary Clinton's email investigation. Another source cited by the journal said that Kushner believed Comey's handling of the Clinton investigation proved he was too unpredictable.

In an email, Robert Ray, former Whitewater independent counsel, said, "A panoply of innocent reasons for wanting to remove an FBI Director that you concluded was 'unpredictable.' The Government would have trouble proving beyond a reasonable doubt that one of those innocent reasons does not explain why the President decided to replace Director Comey, which the chief executive is absolutely entitled to do for any reason, or for no reason at all — so long as that reason does not constitute a knowing and willful attempt to obstruct justice."

A 108-page report published by the Brookings Institution found that However, the president's lawyers have.

Donald Trump offered some insights into his decision. The day after he fired Comey, the president told NBC News, *"regardless of recommendation, I was going to fire Comey."* According to a New York Times report, later in the Oval Office, Trump told Russian officials that firing Comey had relieved enormous pressure on him.

Kushner's Statement

The 11-page statement that Kushner issued to settle the claims against him was the first public accounting of his interactions with Russians while the presidential campaign was going on. Here are the highlights from his statements:

- Kushner admitted that he had four contacts with Russians the year before the presidential campaign. He listed all four of them. The first was a handshake with Sergey Kislyak. The second contact was what stirred a controversy when he met with a Russian lawyer at Trump Tower in the month of June. The third was a meeting he had with Kislyak during the transition. The fourth contact was a meeting he had with the Russian state-run banker Sergey Gorkov during the transition.

- All of these four interactions were already known from previous news reports.

However, Kushner added a few new details in the statement he gave. He talked about the exchange of relevant emails and logistics as well with his Russian acquaintances.

- According to Kushner, none of these interactions were about election interference or collusion. He said, *"I did not collude, nor know of anyone else in the campaign who colluded, with any foreign government."*

- Kushner said he did not read the full email that was forwarded to him by Donald Trump Jr. before he met Kislyak at Trump Tower. That email was to brief him about the Russian lawyer wanting to comply with the Trump campaign officials and give them essential information from the Kremlin. That information was to hurt Hillary Clinton's campaign.

- Kushner further said in his statement that

he was late for the meeting and was there in the room only for 10 minutes while the issue of Russian adoptions was discussed. According to the statement, Kushner had emailed an assistant, requesting him to call him on his cellphone so that he would have an excuse to walk out of the meeting. In his defense, Kushner did not release that email publicly, but he provided it to the intelligence committees.

- Kushner denied a Reuters report that accused him of talking to Kislyak twice on the phone during the presidential campaign. The said Reuters report cited seven unnamed sources who said Kushner did have a conversation with Kisylak on the phone at least twice between April and November of 2016. Kushner's lawyers had already denied the story when it came out in May 2016. Kushner said, "I checked some of my phone records, and my team has not found any calls to any number known to be associated with Ambassador Kislyak."

- Kushner made clear what he discussed in his meeting with Kislyak on December 1, 2016. He said he didn't attempt to create a *"secret back channel"* between the Kremlin and the Trump transition. However, he acknowledged asking Kislyak, *"If they had an existing communication channel at his embassy, we could use where they would be comfortable transmitting sensitive military information about Syria with the Trump transition."* Kislyak could not honor that request, so they did not discuss the idea further.

- Kushner admitted in his statement that Kislyak encouraged him to meet with Sergey Gorkov. He stated he agreed to do that *"because the ambassador had been so insistent."* According to Kushner, one of the most important things he discussed with Gorkov at length was improving US-Russia relations, and he did not talk about *"any private business of any kind."* This clarification contradicted the statement given by a Kremlin spokesman, who said the meeting was a business meeting and that Gorkov met with Kushner in his capacity as *"the head of Kushner Companies,"* not as a member of the incoming administration.

- In his lengthy statement, Kushner admitted shaking hands with Kislyak before Trump made his speech at the Mayflower Hotel in April of 2016. This event triggered scrutiny from investigators on Capitol Hill, who were inclined to determine the extent of Attorney General Jeff Sessions' interactions with Kislyak on the same day.

- The biggest thing that Kushner admitted was that he did receive an email one week before the election from someone he did not recognize. The sender was called *"Guccifer400"*. The email contained an open threat to release Trump's tax returns unless Kushner paid hush money, Kushner said he ignored the email after consulting the issue with a Secret Service agent. The American government said that Russia created an online persona named Guccifer 2.0 as a platform to release emails the Russian intelligence stole during the campaign. However, there is no evidence that Guccifer400 was part of the meddling efforts carried out by the Russian government.

Jared Kushner is believed to be an accomplice in the endeavors of Trump's administration. Making sure that his father-in-law's agendas are seen to and dealt with seems to be his only prerogative. One of the facts that cast doubt on Kushner's political stature is that he didn't include his Russian contacts while submitting a form for security clearance.

Therefore, the FBI did not give Kushner top-secret security clearance. Two career White House security specialists first rejected his application for a top-secret clearance after an FBI background check raised concerns about potential foreign influence on him. However, later, the specialists' supervisor overruled the recommendation and approved Kushner's clearance.

CHAPTER ELEVEN

—·—

JAMES COMEY

THE DISMISSAL OF FBI director James Comey came as a shock and raised several questions. In the days after Trump fired James Comey, law enforcement officials became so concerned about the president's behavior that they started investigating whether he had been working for Russia against American interests or not.

The inquiry conducted by the FBI carried explosive implications. Counterintelligence investigators had to consider whether or not Trump's actions constituted a possible threat to national security. The agents were determined to figure out if the president was deliberately working for the Russian government or had unintentionally fallen under Moscow's influence.

An important thing about the investigation carried out by the FBI was its criminal aspect, which has long been out in public. The criminal element was related to whether Trump's firing of James Comey constituted obstruction of justice or not. The senior FBI officials and agents had grown suspicious of Trump's ties to Russia during the 2016 campaign but chose not to initiate an investigation because they were not sure how to proceed with an inquiry of such magnitude and sensitivity. However, the agents and officials were forced to change their minds after they pondered over the president's activities before and after firing James Comey in May 2017. There were two particular instances in which Trump tied the dismissal of Comey to the Russia investigation, and that prompted the counterintelligence aspect of the examination.

FBI Investigation That Followed James Comey's Dismissal

The special counsel, Robert S. Mueller, took charge of the inquiry into Trump when he was appointed. It was days after FBI officials opened the investigation. That inquiry was part of Mueller's broader examination of how Russian operatives interfered in the 2016 election and whether or not any of Trump's associates conspired with them.

According to James A. Baker, who served as FBI general counsel until late 2017, If Donald Trump had fired James Comey to avoid or put a stop to the Russia investigation. This action would have been rendered as a national security issue because it would have naturally hurt the FBI's effort to learn how Moscow interfered in the 2016 election. Baker privately testified before House investigators who were examining the FBI's handling of the complete Russia inquiry.

"Not only would it be an issue of obstructing an investigation, but the obstruction itself would hurt our

ability to figure out what the Russians had done, and that is what would be the threat to national security," Baker said.

No substantial evidence emerged that Trump was secretly in touch with or took directions from Russian government officials. When an FBI spokeswoman and a spokesman for the special counsel's office were asked if they found any evidence, they both declined.

A lawyer for President Trump, Rudolph W. Giuliani, tried to play down the importance of the investigation by saying,

"The fact that it goes back a year and a half and nothing came of it that showed a breach of national security means they found nothing." At the same time, he acknowledged he had no insight into the ongoing inquiry. The decision to investigate Trump was an aggressive move by FBI officials because they were dealing with the chaotic aftermath of Trump firing Comey and verbally assaulting the Russia investigation by calling it a 'witch hunt.' As a result

of this inquiry, a vigorous debate began between some former law enforcement officials who were not on the case whether FBI officials overreacted in opening the counterintelligence inquiry during a tough period at the Justice Department or not. Other former officials said that those critics were not privy to all of the evidence and sitting on it would have been an apparent abandonment of duty.

The Factors That Triggered the Investigation

Donald Trump caught the attention of FBI counterintelligence agents when he blatantly requested the Russian government during a campaign news conference in July 2016 of his opponent Hillary Clinton. Trump had refused to criticize Russia on the campaign trail and his political moves. Investigators had watched in shock as its convention platform on the Ukraine crisis in a way that seemed to benefit Russia.

Besides that, there was another factor that fueled the FBI's concerns. Christopher Steele, known to the world as a former British spy who worked as an FBI informant, had compiled memos in mid-2016. Those memos contained unsubstantiated claims that Russian officials tried to obtain influence over Trump by preparing a scheme to blackmail and bribe him.

Finally, when Trump, a newly inaugurated president, sought a loyalty pledge from Comey and then asked him to quit his investigation into the president's national security advisor, FBI officials took those requests seriously and initiated discussions to open an inquiry into whether Trump had tried to obstruct the case.

Even when there were several reasons to put FBI officials in doubt about Trump, they chose not to open the investigation until they learned more. As for a counterintelligence inquiry, which involves explicitly fact-finding missions to understand what a foreign power is trying to do and to stop any anti-American activity, FBI officials thought they would need strong evidence to take a step as sensitive as investigating the president. Of course, they were concerned that the perpetration of such an inquiry would be leaked to the news media and would become a global sensation. After all, this wasn't just an ordinary criminal investigation that would result in arrests and convictions. After Comey was fired on May 9, 2017, two more of Trump's actions triggered FBI officials to look into the matter. The first action was Trump writing a letter to Comey about his dismissal, but failing to send it. The letter mentioned the Russia investigation. Trump had thanked Comey for previously telling him he was not a subject of the FBI's ongoing Russia investigation.

The deputy attorney general, Rod J. Rosenstein, wrote a more restrained draft of the letter and told the president that there was no need to mention the Russia investigation in it. He had explained to Trump that Comey's poor handling of the

Clinton email investigation would be enough to have him fired. However, the president ordered Rosenstein to mention the Russia investigation in the letter anyway. Rosenstein disregarded the president's order, which irritated Trump a great deal. Ultimately, the president added a reference to the Russia investigation in the note he delivered, thanking Comey for informing him thrice that he wasn't under investigation. The second event that further prompted FBI investigators was an interview that aired on NBC News, two days after Comey was fired. In the interview, Trump brazenly stated he had fired Comey because of the Russia inquiry.

"I was going to fire Comey knowing there was no good time to do it," Trump said. *"And in fact, when I decided to just do it, I said to myself — I said, you know, this Russia thing with Trump and Russia is a made-up story. It's an excuse by the Democrats for having lost an election that they should've won."*

The aides of Donald Trump said that a proper and fuller examination of his comment demonstrates that he did not fire Comey to end the Russia inquiry. He said,

"I might even lengthen out the investigation, but I have to do the right thing for the American people." Trump further added. "He's the wrong man for that position."

As FBI officials went on debating whether or not to open the investigation into Trump's actions, some of them moved very quickly before Trump could appoint a director who would slow down or even end their investigation into Russia's interference. Moreover, there were many officials involved in the case who viewed Russia as the chief threat to the democratic values of America.

"With respect to Western ideals and who it is and what it is we stand for as Americans, Russia poses the most dangerous threat to that way of life," Lisa Page, a former bureau lawyer, told investigators for a joint House Judiciary and Oversight Committee investigation into Moscow's election interference.

FBI officials considered their decision to act and initiate the investigation quickly as validated when the president commented on visiting Russian officials in the Oval Office soon after firing Comey.

"I just fired the head of the FBI. He was crazy, a real nut job." Trump said, according to a document that summarized the meeting. "I faced great pressure because of Russia. That's taken off."

Four Americans with Ties to Trump and Russia

The months before the 2016 election, the FBI had already caught the scent of Trump's association with Putin and the Kremlin. FBI officials were already investigating four of Trump's associates over their suspicious ties to Russia. The pattern of events made the officials anxious, as they were simultaneously watching Russia's master plan to undermine the presidential election unfold before their eyes. Russia's campaign involved exploiting the existing divisions among Americans for its benefit.

James Comey kept on dodging the questions about the Russia investigation that special counsel Robert Mueller took over, but he did provide some new insight into the ongoing investigation. According to Comey, the FBI's counterintelligence investigation into possible ties between Russia and the Trump campaign originated with 4 Americans who were thought to be assisting the Kremlin in its efforts to intervene in the 2016 election.

Comey did not identify the 4 Americans. He said the identity of these people was not to be disclosed by the FBI publicly. However, Comey mentioned that these four people were Americans and had some connection to Trump during the summer of 2016 and tied to *"the Russian interference effort."* Initially, the investigation started at the end of July 2016. Back then, Comey was not investigating Trump or his campaign, but preferably four Americans.

Steele Dossier

James Comey dealt with the criticism about the start of the FBI's investigation. He argued that the controversial dossier by British spy Christopher Steele was not what convinced them to initiate the investigation. He also clarified that it wasn't the dossier that led the agents to request a surveillance warrant for Carter Page, who at the time was working as a foreign policy aide on Trump's campaign.

Comey further stated, *"The "basis" for the start of the FBI's investigation was information we'd received about a conversation that a Trump campaign foreign policy adviser had with an individual in London about stolen emails that the Russians had that would be harmful to Hillary Clinton." Comey added, "It was weeks or months later that the so-called Steele dossier came to our attention."*

The said London meeting was the one arranged by George Papadopoulos, who was one of several connected to Trump's campaign who have been charged in the investigation.

The dossier went on to make six significant claims about Trump's ties to Russia.

- Trump had cooperated with the Russian authorities for years. A major claim of the dossier is that Russia had been giving Trump and his team valuable intelligence on his opponents, including Hillary Clinton for several years before 2016. And in exchange, Trump's team delivered the Kremlin intelligence on Russian oligarchs and their families for at least eight years.

- Trump is vulnerable to Russian blackmail on sexual matters because he hired prostitutes in Moscow Ritz-Carlton to perform a golden shower show in front of him and Russian intelligence had taped it.

- There was a *"well-developed conspiracy of cooperation"* between Trump and Russia.

- Trump's team knew and approved of

Russian plans to deliver emails to WikiLeaks, and offered them policy concessions in exchange.

- Carter Page, an American consultant, played a crucial role in the conspiracy. He conceived and promoted the idea that the DNC emails should be leaked during the Democratic convention *to swing supporters of Bernie Sanders away from Hilary Clinton and across from Trump.*

- Michael Cohen, a lawyer for Trump, played a vital role in the conspiracy. He traveled to an EU country (most probably the Czech Republic) in late August to meet with Russian officials, and that the meeting took place under the cover of a Russian NGO. One topic of this meeting was *"cover-up and damage limitation"* around Manafort's Ukrainian work and efforts to *"prevent the full details of Trump's relationship with*

Russia being exposed." According to the dossier, after August, Cohen continued to manage Trump's relations with Russia, but contacts were made with Russia's trusted agents instead of officials.

None of these claims has been proven to date.

Comey and Trump Private Meetings and Memos

That is perhaps the turning point in the entire Russia investigation or what the president calls *"this Russia thing."* Before Donald Trump decided to fire James Comey, he met with him on at least two occasions to discuss the then-ongoing FBI investigation of the Trump campaign. However, Trump's version of what was addressed in those private meetings differs from the accounts offered by Comey and people close to him. Based on the leaked memos written by Comey, here's a brief highlight of what happened in those meetings. It's easy to see how Comey's narrative conflicts with Trump's account.

- Trump and Comey met for dinner at the White House on January 27, 2017. According to Trump, Comey asked for the dinner because he wanted to stay on as FBI director. However, the former director of national intelligence said he was told by James Comey that Trump requested the meeting and that Comey was seemingly uneasy with it.

- At the White House dinner, Trump allegedly asked Comey to pledge loyalty to him. That's according to a *New York Times* story that quoted several people close to Comey. On the other hand, Trump denied that account. He said, *"No. No, I didn't. But I don't think it would be a bad question to ask."*

- Trump went on to claim that Comey told him at that dinner and also on two other occasions that he was not under investigation. However, Comey's associates denied that openly. *"That is literally farcical,"* one of Comey's associates told *The Wall Street Journal*.

- Trump said he knows that he is not under investigation because a person under investigation is giving all sorts of documents. However, a person could be under federal investigation without even knowing about it, a former federal prosecutor told us.

- On February 14, 2017, Trump allegedly asked Comey to end the FBI investigation of Michael Flynn, who had resigned a day earlier as the president's national security adviser. According to *The New York Times,* that account is based on a memo that Comey wrote of the meeting. However, the White House said, *"The memo is not a truthful or accurate portrayal of their conversation."*

At the point when the memos were leaked, nobody knew who was telling the truth. Comey was expected to testify before Congress in the future. Thus, it was up to his testimony and the ongoing work of the House and Senate intelligence committees to help clarify these conflicting accounts.

James Comey's Take on Trump in His Public Testimony

The former FBI chief said in his testimony, the transcript of which is 235 pages, *"We have become numb to lying and attacks on the rule of law by the president."* He criticized Trump's contention, in light of the cases of Manafort, Cohen, and other former aides, that it should be a crime for subjects to *"flip"* and cooperate with investigators.

Comey aimed Trump's public insults at the criminal justice system and criticized him further by saying, *"It's a shocking suggestion coming from any senior official, no less the president. It's a critical and legitimate part of the entire justice system in the United States."*

Comey also took his time before the lawmakers to talk about issues, such as Clinton's funding of the dossier, and two FBI employees, Peter Strzok and FBI lawyer Lisa Page, who traded anti-Trump text messages, which raised suspicion of bias in the Russia investigation.

In one of the messages exchanged between the accused FBI employees, Lisa had asked, "[Trump's] not ever going to become president, right? Right?!"

To which, Strzok had replied: "No. No, he's not. We'll stop it."

"Let me be clear, unequivocally and under oath," Strzok said in his opening statement, "not once in my 26 years of defending my nation did my personal opinions impact any official action I took."

In his hearing, Strzok categorically claimed, "I have the utmost respect for Congress's oversight role, but I truly believe that today's hearing is just another victory notch in Putin's belt and another milestone in our enemies' campaign to tear America apart."

In his testimony, Comey cast doubt on Trump's public assertions that Comey was best friends with Mueller. He said, *"I admire the heck out of the man, but I don't know his phone number, I've never been to his house, I don't know his children's names. I think I had a meal once alone with him in a restaurant. I like him. I am not a – I'm an associate of his who admires him greatly. We're not friends in any social sense."*

Comey added he had "never hugged or kissed the man" despite comments made by Trump in the past.

"A relief to my wife," Comey said.

Comey Exonerates Trump of Obstruction of Justice

In his public testimony, Comey exonerated Trump of obstruction of justice. The fired FBI director recounted how Trump expressed compassion as he dismissed him as his National Security Advisor. He had said to Comey that Michael Flynn was a good guy who has been through a lot. Comey agreed to that. Then, according to Comey, the president said, *"I hope you can see your way clear to letting this go, to letting Flynn go."*

Intelligence Committee Chairman, Sen. Richard Burr, R-N.C., asked Comey quite directly, "Was the president trying to obstruct justice?" As expected, Comey demurred by claiming, "It's not for me to say." While there is no legal basis for declining to answer the pivotal question, Comey dodged it for a reason. If he said, under oath, that he regarded the president's words as obstruction, Comey would have incriminated himself in a crime known as "misprision of a felony."

The most stunning moment in Comey's lengthy testimony was when he confessed to leaking the memos to the media. Comey said he deliberately leaked to a friend the contents of the memos that memorialized his conversation with Trump to have them leaked to the press. Comey said it was his personal property, which was wrong. *Under the Federal Records Act and the FBI's Records*

Management regulations, "any document that is made in the course of business" is the property not of the person who authored it, but the property of the U.S. government. And so are its contents. It matters not whether the document, as this one, is unclassified. That means Comey unfittingly and, perhaps, unlawfully leaked a government document that involved an FBI investigation. At the very least, Comey did violate government rules by converting government property for his use.

Under 18 USC 793 (*"Leaking Non-Classified Information"*), it is a crime that is punishable by up to 10 years imprisonment to *"willfully communicate or transmit national defense information,"* even though the information is not classified. While the contents of the leaked memo did not directly deal with national defense matters, the overall investigation did. So, it was debatable whether Comey could be charged.

Many unanimously agreed that Comey's leak appeared to be a somewhat sleazy tactic that was intentionally designed to harm Trump. In many people's opinion, it was disgraceful that Comey purposefully wrote his memo as an unclassified document so that he could later use it to his advantage by leaking it to the public without committing a serious crime.

The Republicans said Comey manipulated the classification system to exploit the political damage his document might cause.

Comey's testimony managed to extinguish the constant accusation that Trump attempted to stop the Russian investigation. Sen. Burr inquired, "Did the president at any time ask you to stop the FBI investigation into Russian involvement in the 2016 U.S. elections?" Comey replied, "Not to my understanding, no."

To many, it seemed Comey branded the president a liar and claimed that Trump defamed him when he described the FBI as "poorly led and in disarray" under Comey's leadership.

As a result, recently, Donald Trump has called for James Comey to be jailed, he has accused him of revealing classified information and of lying to Congress.

CHAPTER TWELVE

— · —

FACEBOOK

SENATOR MARK WARNER, THE top Democrat on the Senate intelligence committee, said that Facebook officials informed Senate staff that the ads purchased by Russians were geared toward urging users to *"like"* certain political groups. That resulted in political messages flooding their Facebook news feeds

"This is kind of a whole ecosystem, where you have ads are one component, but then you have accounts, and if those accounts, like a certain group ... 'Mark Warner for Senate,' whatever, pops up much higher in your newsfeed. And you as a person don't screen that." Warner said.

According to Facebook's chief security officer, Russian trolls purchased over $100,000 in ads over the last two years. These purchased ads included a handful of advertisements, which specifically mentioned the names, Donald Trump and Hillary Clinton. A congressional source, who was familiar with the Facebook briefings, said that the idea behind purchasing the ads was not to influence Facebook users directly to vote for one candidate or favor one candidate over another based on the ads. Instead, the scheme was to plug the users into groups and then flood their feeds with politically charged messages to influence their actions.

"Mentioning a specific candidate is only one way to attract a vote, or more importantly, and I think in many cases this was about voter suppression," Warner said. "So you can raise an issue without mentioning a candidate."

According to Warner, Facebook officials refused to provide the committee with any copies of documents. They did not hand over committee staff anything in their briefing.

A Few Important Facts about the Ads

When asked what was in the ads that were shared with Congress and how many people saw those ads, here's what Facebook officials had to say:

"Most of the ads appear to focus on divisive social and political messages across the ideological spectrum, touching on topics from LGBT matters to race issues to immigration to gun rights. A number of them appear to encourage people to follow Pages on these issues."

Here are a few other facts about the ads:

Facebook's Response to the Ads

- It is estimated that almost 10 million people in America saw the ads. The Facebook officials were able to approximate the number of people who were exposed to at least one of these ads by using their best modeling.

- 44% of total ads were before the 2016 US election, and 56% were after the election.

- It is estimated that 25% of the ads were never shown to anyone. That's because advertising auctions are designed based on relevance, and certain ads may not reach anyone as a result.

- Less than $3 was spent on 50% of the ads, and less than $1,000 were spent on 99% of the ads.

- Out of more than 3,000 ads that Facebook shared with Congress, 5% appeared on Instagram. It is estimated that $6,700 was spent on these ads.

Facebook officials reported that some of the ads were paid for in Rubles. However, they said that currency alone is not a very good way to identify suspicious activity because the majority of advertisers who pay in Russian currency aren't doing anything wrong. According to the officials, they did use the currency as a signal to identify these ads, but it wasn't the only signal. Facebook officials stated that they were inclined to refine their techniques to determine the kind of ads in question. They refrained from providing any further details because that would give bad actors a roadmap for avoiding future detection.

Facebook officials said that the 2016 US elections were the first time where evidence was widely reported against foreign actors who exploited the internet to influence voter behavior. The officials went on to say that they know how their service was abused and promised to investigate to learn all they could. They added, *"We know that our experience is only a small piece of a much larger puzzle. Congress and the special counsel are best placed to put these pieces together because they have much broader investigative power to obtain information from other sources."*

Facebook, after an extensive and careful legal and policy review, concluded that they should share the ads with Congress in a manner that is consistent with their obligations to protect user information. They decided to assist government authorities in trying to figure out what happened in the 2016 elections. Since federal law places strict restrictions on disclosing account information, thus Facebook didn't make any such information public. The officials said, *"Given the sensitive national security and privacy issues involved in this extraordinary investigation, we think Congress is best placed to use the information we and others provide to inform the public comprehensively and completely."*

When asked if Facebook had any idea that the purchased ads might be part of a Russian operation, the officials clearly stated that they didn't know. Here's what they had to say:

"The vast majority of our over 5 million advertisers use our self-service tools. This allows individuals or businesses to create a Facebook page, attach a credit card or some other payment method and run ads promoting their posts."

The officials further added:

"In reviewing the ads buys, we have found approximately $100,000 in ad spending from June of 2015 to May of 2017 — associated with roughly 3,000 ads — that was connected to about 470 inauthentic accounts and Pages in violation of our policies. Our analysis suggests these accounts and Pages were affiliated with one another and likely operated out of Russia."

Facebook officials made it very clear that in some situations, their employees work directly with their advertisers. However, in the case of Russian ads, none of the employees was found to be involved in direct relationships.

Cambridge Analytica Employee Whistleblower

The data analytics firm that worked with Trump's election team and the winning Brexit campaign harvested millions of Facebook profiles of American voters. That is termed one of the tech giant's most significant data breaches. The data collected in the violation was then used to develop a powerful software program to influence and predict the choices of people at the ballot box.

A whistleblower revealed how Cambridge Analytica – a company owned by the hedge fund billionaire Robert Mercer, and headed at the time by Trump's principal advisor, Steve Bannon – used personal information taken without authorization in early 2014 to build a system that could profile individual US voters. The intention was to target individual voters with personalized political advertisements.

Christopher Wylie, who worked with a Cambridge University academic to obtain the data, said, "We exploited Facebook to harvest millions of people's profiles. And built models to exploit what we knew about them and target their inner demons. That was the basis the entire company was built on."

As confirmed by a Facebook statement, by late 2015 the company had found out that information was harvested on an unprecedented scale. However, it was too late for the company to alert users, and was able to take only limited steps to recover and secure the private information of more than 50 million individuals.

It revealed that the data was collected with the help of an app called *"thisisyourdigitallife."* The app was reportedly developed by academic Aleksandr Kogan separately from his work spot at Cambridge University. In the beginning, when Kogan developed the app, he, through his company Global Science Research (GSR) and in collaboration with Cambridge Analytica, paid hundreds of thousands of users to take a personality test and share their data for educational use. The app in question also collected information about the test-takers Facebook friends, which led to the accumulation of a data pool. Facebook's platform policy only allowed the collection of friends' data to improve user experience in the app. The company didn't allow for selling the information or for advertising purposes. The discovery of the unmatched data harvesting and the use to which it was put raised new and urgent questions about Facebook's role in targeting voters in the 2016 US presidential election.

Facebook and Cambridge Analytica happened to be a focus of an inquiry into data and politics by the British Information Commissioner's Office. According to information commissioner Elizabeth Denham, *"We are investigating the circumstances in which Facebook data may have been illegally acquired and used. It's part of our ongoing investigation into the use of data analytics for political purposes which was launched to consider how political parties and campaigns, data analytics companies, and social media platforms in the UK are using and analyzing people's personal information to micro-target voters."*

The revelations about the breach and the purpose for which the harvested data was used incited widespread outrage. As a result, Massachusetts Attorney General Maura Healey announced that the state would be conducting an investigation.

"Residents deserve answers immediately from Facebook and Cambridge Analytica." She tweeted.

After more than two years of a data breach, Facebook announced it was suspending Cambridge Analytica and Kogan from the platform.

Senator Mark Warner said that harvesting data on such a large scale for political targeting highlighted the need for Congress to improve controls. He proposed an Honest Ads Act which would regulate online political advertising in the same way as television, print, and radio.

"This story is more evidence that the online political advertising market is essentially the Wild West. Whether it's allowing Russians to purchase political ads or extensive micro-targeting based on ill-gotten user data, it's clear that if left unregulated, this market will continue to be prone to deception and lacking in transparency." Warner said.

The CEO of Cambridge Analytica, Alexander Nix, told a parliamentary inquiry that the company did not have nor used private Facebook data. When

Simon Milner, Facebook's UK policy director, was asked if Cambridge Analytica was in possession of Facebook data, he told MPs, *"They may have lots of data, but it will not be Facebook user data. It may be data about people who are on Facebook that they have gathered themselves, but it is not data that we have provided."*

Still, in his testimony, Alexander Nix went on to say, "We do not work with Facebook data, and we do not have Facebook data."

Wylie, a Canadian data analytics expert who worked with Kogan and Cambridge Analytica to devise and implement the data harvest scheme, showed a dossier of evidence about the data misuse. The record, which includes emails, invoices, contracts, and bank transfers, raised questions about Nix's testimony and revealed more than 50 million profiles belonging to registered American voters. These were the voters whose data was harvested from the site in one of the largest-ever breaches of Facebook data.

Despite his role as a whistleblower, Facebook ended up suspending Wylie from accessing the platform as it continued to carry out its investigation. When the breach happened, Wylie was a Cambridge Analytica employee. However, Facebook claimed he was working for Eunoia Technologies, a company he set up on his own after leaving his former employer in late 2014.

The Letter from Facebook

The evidence Wylie gave to the UK and US authorities also included a letter from Facebook's lawyers that was sent to him in August 2016. It requested Wylie to destroy any data he held that had been collected by GSR, and the company set up by Kogan to harvest the profiles.

"Because this data was obtained and used without permission, and because GSR was not authorized to share or sell it to you, it cannot be used legitimately in the future and must be deleted immediately." The letter said.

The letter went unanswered for a very long time because Wylie was traveling at the time. However, Facebook did not pursue a response from him and did not ensure that he deleted the harvested data. Here's what Wylie said:

"That, to me, was the most astonishing thing. They waited two years and did absolutely nothing to check that the data was deleted. All they asked me to do was tick a box on a form and post it back."

Paul-Olivier Dehaye, a data protection specialist, who headed the investigative efforts into the tech giant, said, "Facebook has denied and denied and denied this. It has misled MPs and congressional investigators, and it's failed in its duties to respect the law. It has a legal obligation to inform regulators and individuals about this data breach, and it hasn't. It's failed time and time again to be open and transparent."

The fact of the matter is that a majority of American states have laws that require notification in some cases of a data breach. California, where

Facebook is based, happens to be one of those states. However, Facebook never stopped denying that the harvesting of tens of millions of profiles by GSR and Cambridge Analytica was a data breach. It refused to accept that there was a flaw in its system, which made this data harvest possible. Facebook said in a statement, *"Kogan gained access to this information in a legitimate way and through the proper channels but did not subsequently abide by our rules because he passed the information on to third parties."*

Facebook claimed that it removed the app back in 2015 and required certification from everyone with copies that the data destroyed. According to the company, it didn't make a difference if the letter to Wylie was sent until the second half of 2016. Here's what Paul Grewal, Facebook's vice president, said in a statement:

"We are committed to vigorously enforcing our policies to protect people's information. We will take whatever steps are required to see that this happens."

It is said Facebook then began investigating reports that suggest not all data had been deleted. Eventually, it was revealed that Kogan had previously unreported links to a Russian university and took Russian grants for research. He had a license from Facebook to collect profile data, but it was for research purposes only. So when he gathered the information for the commercial venture, he was violating the company's terms. Kogan continues to say that everything he did was legal, and says he had a close working relationship with Facebook, which had granted him permission for his apps.

The Contract and a Powerful Political Tool

A contract dated 4 June 2014 confirms that SCL, an affiliate of Cambridge Analytica, entered into a commercial arrangement with GSR. The agreement mentions harvesting and processing Facebook data. The Observer has seen the said contract. It noted that Cambridge Analytica spent almost $1 million on data collection and obtained more than 50 million individual profiles that could match electoral rolls.

The stolen data was then used to develop a program that could analyze Facebook profiles and determine personality traits associated with voting behavior. The algorithm and database together created a powerful political tool. It allowed a campaign to identify possible swing voters and craft messages that likely resonated with them.

"The ultimate product of the training set is creating a gold standard of understanding personality from Facebook profile information." The contract specifies. It also promises to create a database of 2 million matched profiles, identifiable and tied to electoral registers, across 11 states, but with room to expand much further.

At that time, 50 million profiles represented one-third of active North American Facebook users and nearly a quarter of potential American voters. When MPs asked Nix if any of his company's data had come from GSR, he said, *"We had a relationship with GSR. They did some research for us back in 2014. That research proved to be fruitless, and so the answer is no."*

A representative of Cambridge Analytica stated that the company's contract with GSR stipulated that Kogan should seek consent for data collection and that there was no reason to believe why he wouldn't do that.

SCL worked with Facebook to make sure no terms were knowingly breached and gave a signed statement to ensure that all data have been deleted. Cambridge Analytica also asserted that none of the data has been used in the 2016 US election.

Throughout the case, Steve Bannon's lawyer made no comment because he said his client "knows nothing about the claims being asserted". He added, "The first time Mr. Bannon heard of these reports was from media inquiries in the past few days."

Thus, Bannon's lawyer directed inquiries to Alexander Nix.

The Lawmakers and Zuckerberg

House members took turns to grill Facebook CEO Mark Zuckerberg regarding the failure of the most popular social media networking site to protect the personal information of about 87 million users. They called the billionaire to explain the shocking reports about data security issues and requested he help fix the problems.

Zuckerberg testified before the committee on Capitol Hill before a joint hearing of the Senate's commerce and judiciary committees. Here's what Zuckerberg said during their testimony before the House commerce committee:

"The internet is growing in importance around the world in people's lives, and I think that it is inevitable that there will need to be some regulation. So my position is not that there should be no regulation, but I also think that you have to be careful about the regulation you put in place."

Instead of putting a dent in Zuckerberg's armor, Facebook shares went up more than 1 percent. Two days of questioning resulted in Zuckerberg restoring more than $25 billion in market value that Facebook lost since the Cambridge Analytica scandal surfaced in mid-March.

The 33-year-old tech tycoon was called in Washington to shed light on how a political data company, Cambridge Analytica, associated with Trump's presidential campaign, was able to get its hands on the personal information of 87 million Facebook users. Zuckerberg met privately with senators and made behind-the-scene apologies.

"Looking back, it's clear we were too slow identifying election interference in 2016, and we need to do better in future elections," Zuckerberg mentioned in an open letter posted on Facebook just minutes before meeting senators privately and promised to fix issues with Facebook.

Zuckerberg said in his well-prepared and well-rehearsed House testimony that Facebook is reviewing every single app that might have access to users' data. He added that he locked down the platform to stop developers from selling such sensitive data to companies like Cambridge Analytica.

"I started Facebook. I run it. I'm responsible for what happens there." Zuckerberg told the packed hearing room.

Zuckerberg also assured that Facebook is developing artificial intelligence that would be able to detect hate speech and verify every political advertiser. He said the company had already improved on flagging misinformation or identifying fake accounts and doubtful activities since the 2016 elections when Russians bought almost $100,000 worth of Facebook ads.

"But it's an arms race," Zuckerberg said in *reference to online attempts made to disrupt elections worldwide. "They're going to keep getting better at this, and we need to invest in keeping on getting better at this, too."*

"We know some members of Congress are exploring ways to increase transparency around political or issue

advertising, and we're happy to keep working with Congress on that. But we aren't waiting for legislation to act."

Zuckerberg further added that *"preventing interference and misinformation in the 2018 midterm elections"* is among his top priorities.

Chapter Thirteen

—·—

The Curious Case of Michael Flynn

A LONG WITH OTHER ADVISORS to Donald Trump's campaign during the 2016 U.S. elections, Michael Flynn was also in contact with Russian officials. There were at least 18 calls and emails made during the last seven months of the 2016 presidential election. That was what the U.S. officials familiar with the exchanges told Reuters.

Suspicions against Michael Flynn had risen when he was sighted on December 10 of 2015 sitting next to Russian President Vladimir Putin at a dinner in Moscow. The occasion was the 10th anniversary of the Kremlin-linked English language news service R.T. Later on, Michael Flynn went on record to say that he didn't even talk to the Russian president. However, eventually, it was revealed that Michael Flynn was paid a sum of $45,000 to attend the dinner.

After almost two months, Michael Flynn, the former director of the Defense Intelligence Agency, joined the Trump campaign as an advisor on national security issues. His joining lent heft to Trump's thin list of aides. Then in the final seven months of the presidential campaign, Michael Flynn and his other aides held 18 email and phone conversations with Russian operatives. In the summer of 2016, American spies observed Russian discussions about what would be the optimal way of using the campaign chairman, Paul Manafort, to their advantage.

The controversial exchange of emails and phone calls formed part of the record subject to review by FBI and congressional investigators that were probing Russian interference in the American presidential election and contacts between Trump's campaign and Russia.

Six of the previously unrevealed contacts described to Reuters were telephone calls between Russia's ambassador to the United States Sergei Kislyak and Trump's advisors, including Michael Flynn. The secret conversations between Kislyak and Flynn accelerated after November 8 voting took place. According to four American officials, the two conversed about establishing a backchannel for communication between Putin and Trump that could bypass the U.S. national security bureaucracy, which both sides considered hostile to improved relations.

In January 2017, the Trump administration initially denied any contact with Russian officials during the 2016 election campaign. However, since then, the advisors to the campaign have confirmed four meetings between Trump's advisors and Kislyak during that time. The people who mentioned the contacts said they found no substantial evidence of any illegal activity or collusion between Russia and the campaign in the review of those communications. If disclosed, the details of the said communications could increase the pressure on Trump and his aides to provide Congress and the FBI with a full account of interactions with Russian officials and the Kremlin during and after the 2016 presidential election.

When the White House was requested for comment, the request had met with silence. Michael Flynn's lawyer also declined to pronounce in this regard. In Moscow, an official of the Russian foreign ministry declined to comment on the questionable contacts and referred Reuters to the Trump administration. However, a spokesman for the Russian embassy in Washington stated, *"We do not comment on our daily contacts with the local interlocutors."*

What Were the 18 Phone Calls and Emails About?

The 18 telephone calls and emails that created ripples in the American political landscape took place between April and November of 2016. That was the period when Russian hackers engaged in what US intelligence termed as a Kremlin campaign to harm the reputation of the election and influence its outcome in favor of Trump over the Democratic contender, former secretary of state Hillary Clinton.

According to the sources, the discussions in the emails and over the calls were focused on mending the troubled American-Russian economic relations, which were strained by sanctions imposed on Moscow. Other than that, the discussion was about cooperating in fighting Islamic State in Syria and containing a more assertive China.

An interesting fact that surfaced was that there were another 12 calls, emails, or text messages in addition to the six phone calls made to Kislyak. These 12 calls were between Trump's campaign advisors and Russian officials or the people who were thought to be close to Putin at the time.

One of those calls was by a Ukrainian politician and oligarch Viktor Medvedchuk. This piece of information had given by one person who had in-depth knowledge of the exchange, and two other people also familiar with the issue. Although, it cannot be said confidently, who was Medvedchuk in conversation with Trump's side, the theme of the conversation he had included American-Russian cooperation. For those who don't know, Putin happens to be the godfather to Medvedchuk's daughter.

When Medvedchuk was asked about the exchange, he denied being in conversation with anyone from the Trump campaign. He said in an email to Reuters, *"I am not acquainted with any of Donald Trump's close associates; therefore, no such conversation could have taken place."*

According to the sources, it has further revealed that in the confidential conversations during the campaign, Russian officials laid emphasis on a pragmatic, business-style approach, and tried to convince Trump's associates that they make deals about economic and other interests, and put contentious issues on the side. Veterans of previous election campaigns have come out and have said that although contacts with foreign officials during a presidential election campaign were not unusual at all, the number of communications between Russian officials and Trump aides was an exception.

Richard Armitage, a Republican and former deputy secretary of state, said, "It's rare to have that many phone calls to foreign officials, especially to a country we consider an adversary or a hostile power."

Members of the Senate and House intelligence committees went to the CIA and the National Security Agency to review transcripts and other documents related to contacts between Trump campaign advisers and Russian officials. Eventually, the U.S. Justice Department announced that it had appointed Robert Mueller, a former FBI Director, as special counsel to investigate alleged Russian interference in the US 2016 election and any possible signs of collusion between Russia and Trump's campaign.

Masked & Anonymous Contacts and Confidential Meetings

Other than Bedvedchuk and Kislyak, the identities of Russian officials and different Putin-linked participants, who were in contact with Trump's advisors during the 2016 election, have been kept classified. The names of Trump's advisors, who were in touch, have also been masked in intelligence reports. Because of legal protections for their privacy as US citizens. The only advisor's name that had been mentioned publicly was Michael Flynn. However, if the advisors want, they can request that their identities be revealed for intelligence purposes.

As per routine, the United State and allied intelligence and law enforcement agencies monitored interactions and movements of Russian officials. After Vice President Mike Pence and others denied that the representatives of the Trump campaign had any contact with Russian officials, the White House eventually confirmed that Kislyak indeed met twice with then-Senator Jeff Sessions, who later went on to become attorney general.

Kislyak was also reported to have attended an event in Washington where Trump expressed his desire to seek better relations with Russia. Jared Kushner, Trump's son-in-law, and senior White House adviser, also attended that event. In addition to that event, Kislyak met with two other Trump campaign advisers on the sidelines of the Republican convention.

Trump Dismisses Michael Flynn

Flynn could not definitively refute a Washington Post story that mentioned his conversations with Kislyak included a discussion about the newly imposed sanctions. It was a serious issue because it was illegal for unauthorized private citizens to negotiate with foreign governments on behalf of America.

Flynn's inability to refute the story stirred controversy because it put Vice President Mike Pence and several senior White House advisors in an uncomfortable position. The problem was they had denied in TV interviews weeks earlier that Flynn discussed sanctions with the ambassador. That led some administration officials to believe Flynn must have lied to Pence and others.

Thus, in February 2017, Trump asked for and got Flynn's resignation after it became apparent that he had incorrectly characterized the nature of phone conversations with Kislyak that took place in late December. Promptly after the November 8 election, the Obama administration announced new sanctions on Russia. Michael Flynn offered to testify to Congress and demanded immunity in return from prosecution. However, the House intelligence committee rejected his offer.

Flynn's departure was rooted in the fact that the Justice Department warned the Trump administration that Flynn had misled administration officers about his interactions with Kislyak and was vulnerable to blackmail by the Russians.

According to an obtained by CNN, Flynn wrote, "I inadvertently briefed the Vice President-elect and others with incomplete information regarding my phone calls with the Russian ambassador. I have sincerely apologized to the President and the Vice President, and they have accepted my apology."

"I am tendering my resignation, honored to have served our nation and the American people in such a distinguished way. I know with the strong leadership of President Donald J. Trump and Vice President Mike Pence and the superb team they are assembling, this team will go down in history as one of the greatest presidencies in US history." Flynn added.

The resignation came as a blow to everyone because Flynn quit less than a month into the job. That makes him one of the shortest-serving senior presidential advisers in modern history. The White House concluded that Flynn did not intend to mislead the vice president. However, he may have resigned because he could not exactly remember what he said to the Russians. *The White House said, "Not remembering is not a quality we can have for the national security adviser."*

According to an administration source, Trump 'hung in there when it came to Flynn. However, there was a flood of information that finally made it noticeable he had to resign. It was hard for Trump to let Flynn go. After all, Flynn had counseled Trump on national security and foreign policy matters since early 2016.

Concerns Raised over Flynn's Dismissal

Many raised concerns at the idea that Flynn, who was a retired lieutenant general and headed the Defense Intelligence Agency, would dare to discuss sanctions with the Russian ambassador whose calls are regularly monitored by US intelligence and law enforcement agencies.

An American official confirmed to CNN that, among other matters, Flynn and Kislyak did discuss sanctions during a call in December. After the call was made public, Pence told CBS News that Flynn did not discuss sanctions with Kislyak, which the Obama administration recently imposed owing to Russia's alleged interference in the 2016 elections. *Pence told CBS News, "They did not discuss anything having to do with the United States' decision to expel diplomats or impose censure against Russia."*

A few days later, a source close to the national security adviser told CNN that Flynn could not rule out that he spoke about sanctions on the call.

The FBI Investigation into Flynn's Questionable Actions

A pair of Democratic lawmakers – Representatives John Conyers, Jr., top Democrat on the House Judiciary Committee, and Elijah Cummings, top Democrat on the House oversight committee – sent a request for a 'full classified briefing' on the circumstances surrounding Flynn to the Justice Department and FBI the night following Flynn's resignation.

"We in Congress need to know who authorized his actions, permitted them, and continued to let him have access to our most sensitive national security information despite knowing these risks. We need to know who else within the White House is a current and ongoing risk to our national security." The Democratic lawmakers wrote in a statement. "This new disclosure warrants a full classified briefing by all relevant agencies, including the Department of Justice and the FBI, as soon as possible and certainly before Thursday, February 16. We are communicating this request to the Department of Justice and FBI this evening." They added.

A surprising fact that came to attention was that was under FBI investigation earlier than previously thought. According to a little section, which went unnoticed by most, in Special Counsel Robert Mueller's report and Flynn's brother, Joe Flynn, it was *a long-running, high-level effort to "trip him up" and "trap" him.*

Buried in the was a mention of an existing FBI investigation of Flynn 'based on his relationship with the Russian government,' which predated Flynn's phone calls during the presidential transition in December 2016 with then-Russian ambassador Sergei Kislyak that ultimately led to his termination for lying.

Previously, it assumed that Flynn's interactions with Kislyak, which were picked up by the U.S. intelligence community, were what made the FBI suspicious and sparked the Flynn probe. However, Mueller's report suggests otherwise.

According to, "members of the intelligence community were surprised by Russia's decision not to retaliate in response to the sanctions. When analyzing Russia's response, they became aware of Flynn's discussion of sanctions with Kislyak. Previously, the FBI had opened an investigation of Flynn based on his relationship with the Russian government. Flynn's contacts with Kislyak became a key component of that investigation."

To this day, the FBI has not cleared Michael Flynn.

Michael Flynn Pleaded Guilty

On December 1, 2017, Flynn made a plea bargain which the special counsel agreed to. In the bargain, Flynn pleaded guilty to *willfully and knowingly making false, fictitious, and fraudulent statements* to the FBI regarding his interactions with Russia's ambassador, Kislyak. However, Flynn falsely denied that he had asked Kislyak *'to refrain from escalating ... in response to sanctions that the United States had imposed against Russia that same day.'*

Flynn pleaded guilty and acknowledged that he was cooperating with the investigation by Mueller. He said, "*It has been extraordinarily painful to endure these many months of false accusations of "treason" and other outrageous acts... Such false accusations are contrary to everything I have ever done and stood for. But I recognize that the actions I acknowledged in court today were wrong, and, through my faith in God, I am working to set things right. My guilty plea and agreement to cooperate with the special counsel's office reflect a decision I made in the best interests of my family and of our country. I accept full responsibility for my actions."*

In a sentencing memorandum made public on December 4, 2018, the Mueller investigation stated that Flynn *'deserves credit for accepting responsibility in a timely fashion and substantially assisting the government and should receive little or no jail time.'*

On December 11 of 2018, Michael Flynn's lawyers submitted a sentencing memo, in which they requested leniency for Flynn. They asked a federal judge to spare Flynn prison time. Moreover, the lawyers suggested that FBI agents who interviewed Flynn previously at the White House had tricked him into lying and did not advise him that lying to federal agents is a felony. Flynn's lawyers argued that his contrition, lengthy military service, and willingness to aid Mueller's investigation, should warrant a sentence of only probation. Here's what the lawyers wrote that included letters from Flynn's supporters vouching for his character:

"His cooperation was not grudging or delayed."

However, the lawyers failed to offer a robust and convincing explanation as to why Flynn decided to lie to FBI agents about his conversations with Kislyak during the presidential campaign in late 2016. Even in accepting blame, Flynn tried to come across as a victim of FBI tactics, which according to him, were geared toward trapping him. His lawyers pointed out details from the interview and asserted that Flynn's relaxed behavior during questioning indicated that he was not lying to FBI investigators.

Two days later, Trump tweeted about that assertion, "They convinced him he did lie, and he made some kind of a deal."

Mueller's office boldly contested and rejected these assertions the very next day. They said to refresh his memory, federal agents read brief portions of what Flynn had talked about with

Sergei Kislyak, but Flynn didn't waver from his false statements. Consequently, FBI agents concluded that Flynn's relaxed demeanor during the interview shows nothing but his full commitment to his lies. Therefore, Kremlin could compromise him.

Moreover, Mueller's office also presented instances when Flynn brazenly lied about his conversations with Kislyak during the days before the FBI interview.

The New York Times reported that Flynn's *"decision to attack the FBI in his plea for probation appeared to be a gambit for a pardon from Mr. Trump, whose former lawyer had broached the prospect last year with a lawyer for Mr. Flynn."*

As of now, Flynn's sentencing has been deferred several times. He is still waiting for his sentence in the wake of his guilty plea for misleading FBI investigators about his interactions with the Russian ambassador. His case made it to the headlines once again when prosecutors said in a court filing that *'Flynn had told Mueller's office that people tied to*

Congress and the administration tried to influence his cooperation with the probe.'

Now, the judge has categorically ordered specific sections of Mueller's report to be presented to him unredacted. As for the special counsel's release, it did not reach a pertinent conclusion on whether Trump obstructed justice or not. However, Attorney General Bill Barr and then-deputy Rod Rosenstein have stated that the evidence does not warrant a criminal charge against Michael Flynn."

Chapter Fourteen

— · —

Michael Cohen

M ICHAEL DEAN COHEN IS a former American attorney who served as Donald Trump's lawyer from 2006 until May 2018. Aside from being his lawyer, Cohen was a vice president of The Trump Organization and the personal counsel to the American President. Media often described him as Trump's fixer. It was Cohen with whom President Trump and his company's chief financial officer, Allen Weisselberg, coordinated to pay hush money for the silence of an adult film actress to hide Trump's affair with her. Cohen used sham invoices to cover the whole case up. That was what

Michael Cohen stated in his testimony to the House Oversight Committee.

Also in his testimony, Cohen showed lawmakers a check dated August 1, 2017, that was signed by Trump, his son Donald Jr., and Weisselberg. According to Cohen, this check correlated to the $130,000 payment he made on Trump's orders to a porn star named Stormy Daniels, whose legal name is Stephanie Clifford. These checks were part of monthly installments to reimburse Cohen for paying the porn star just before the 2016 presidential election. In response, Trump lashed out at Cohen on Twitter, saying, *"Michael Cohen...was just disbarred by the State Supreme Court for lying & fraud. He did bad things unrelated to Trump. He is lying to reduce his prison time."* Republicans on the committee didn't refrain from making similar charges against Cohen, who pleaded guilty to lying to Congress back in August 2018, a year after the intro began. Cohen pleaded guilty to 8 counts, including violations, and.

The Payments Cohen Made and Received

Essential Consultants LLC is a Delaware shell company that Cohen established in October 2016 to pay Stormy Daniels. After that, Cohen used the company for a range of shady business activities, which are mostly unknown to the public. It said that Cohen moved $4.4 million through the company between the time of the 2016 election and January 2018. In May 2018, Michael Avenatti, Daniels' lawyer posted a 7-page report on Twitter that had details about the financial transactions involving Essential Consultants and Cohen. At first, Avenatti did not confirm his source. Later, the source was revealed to be The New York Times and other publications. The data showed hundreds and thousands of dollars transferred to Cohen through Essential Consultants from Fortune 500 companies, including Novartis and AT&T, which had business before the Trump administration.

It further revealed that Essential Consultants received at least $500,000 from a firm based in New York called Columbus Nova. The said firm is linked to a Russian Oligarch. The firm's largest client is reportedly a company controlled by Viktor Vekselberg, a Ukrainian-born Russian oligarch.

Once these payments were made public, questions were raised about them, especially four of them that totaled around $200,000 and were paid by AT&T to the Cohen's firm between October 2017 and January 2018. AT&T claimed that the hefty sum of money was paid to Essential Consultants to provide insights into understanding the new administration and that the firm didn't do any legal or lobbying work for AT&T. Cohen was paid $600,000 ($50,000 per month) over the year by AT&T, whose CEO described the payments as a big mistake. Novartis, a Switzerland–based pharmaceutical giant, reportedly paid Cohen almost $1.2 million in separate payments. According to the statement Novartis released, the company hired the

LLC to help it understand the healthcare policy of Trump's administration. However, the company stated it did not receive a benefit for its investment. Similarly, other companies paid hefty amounts of money to the LLC. Korea Aerospace Industries was one of them. The company ostensibly paid $150,000for advice on cost accounting standards.

Franklin Haney Company agreed to pay Cohen $10 million if he successfully lobbied for the United States Department of Energy to finance the Bellefonte Nuclear Generating Station. On August 21, 2018, Cohen pleaded guilty to 8 counts. He professed to have made illegal payments in the coordination and direction of a candidate for federal office.

Michael Cohen's Connection to Russia

According to the Trump-Russia dossier published in January 2017, Cohen met with Russian officials in Prague, the Czech Republic in 2016. As per the source, his objective was to pay those who had hacked the DNC and *"cover up all traces of the hacking operation."* The dossier is said to contain raw intelligence and is believed to be a blend of accurate and inaccurate information. Cohen denied the allegations against him and stated that he never went to Prague. He said, he was in Los Angeles between August 23 and 29, and that he spent the entire month of September in New York.

When Czech intelligence sources were asked, they reported there were no records of Cohen entering Prague by plane. However, Respekt magazine and Politico put forward a theory that said he could have come to the Czech capital by car or train from a neighboring country, for example, Italy.

In April 2018, the DC Bureau of McClatchy Newspapers reported Special Counsel Robert Mueller had evidence that Cohen did travel to Prague, and that two sources confirmed the secret trip. It said that the evidence showed Cohen entered Prague from Germany. Since both countries are in the European Union's Schengen passport area,

Cohen would not need a passport stamp to enter Czech territory.

Cohen denied the allegations and said he didn't even travel to the European Union in August 2016. According to a McClatchy report, mobile phones pinged cellphone towers around Prague in the late summer of 2016. The mobile phone was traced back to Cohen. According to the same statement, an eastern European intelligence agency intercepted communications between Russians. One of the communications mentioned that Cohen was in Prague.

The Mueller Report tends to dismiss all the reports and states *"Cohen had never traveled to Prague and was not concerned about those allegations, which he believed were provably false."*

Cohen is also said to have met with Ukrainian opposition politician Andrey Artemenko and Felix Sater in Manhattan at the Loews Regency to discuss a plan to lift sanctions against Russia. The proposal would require Russian forces to withdraw from

Ukraine, and a referendum to be held in Ukraine on whether Crimea should be leased to Russia for 50 or 100 years. It is said that Cohen received this written proposal in a sealed envelope that was delivered to Michael Flynn, the then-National Security Advisor.

When the inquiries were made into alleged Russian interference in the 2016 presidential election, two congressional panels required Cohen to provide information about any interactions he had with people associated with the Russian government. Cohen was a subject of the Mueller investigation in 2018, and he cooperated with Mueller's team for a decreased sentence. On December 12, 2018, Cohen was sentenced to three years in prison and a $50,000 fine. Besides, Cohen was ordered to pay $1.4 million in restitution and forfeit $500,000. At his sentence hearing,

Cohen said, *"I take full responsibility for each act that I pled guilty to The personal ones to me and those involving the president of the United States of America."* Cohen further referred to Trump as *"the man that caused me to choose the path of darkness and do dirty deeds."*

Before passing the sentence, the judge said, "Each of these crimes is a serious offense against the United States. Mr. Cohen pled guilty to a veritable smorgasbord of fraudulent conduct."

Cohen's Testimony before Three Congressional Committees

After scheduling conflicts and delays, Cohen testified before three congressional committees in late February. The first testimony was on February 26, 2019; It was a closed-door hearing before the Senate Intelligence Committee. Cohen testified for more than seven hours. The second testimony was on February 27, 2019, where Cohen gave 10 hours of testimony, which was aired and televised. This testimony was before the House Oversight Committee, during which Cohen described Trump as a 'racist,' a 'con man,' and a 'cheat.'

He also went on to express his shame and remorse for the things he had done under Trump's influence on him. He clarified that the president reimbursed him for all the illegal hush-money payments, and suggested that he should lie to Congress about the Trump Tower Moscow negotiations. He further confessed that he filed false financial statements with insurance companies and banks.

In what is known as a remarkable spectacle of a testimony, Cohen came up with fresh allegations against Trump and his administration oath. These allegations surely took the legal, political, and media worlds by storm. Cohen confessed that Trump knew ahead of time that WikiLeaks was about to dump Democratic National Committee emails that were damaging to his presidential candidate, Hillary Clinton. He further confessed that Trump continued to discuss his plans to build a Trump Tower in Moscow throughout 2016. This revelation contradicted Cohen's testimony before Congress back in 2017 where he said the project ended in January 2016.

Cohen said Trump must have asked him at least six times between January and June of 2016 how the Moscow project was going. Cohen also brought to attention that he discussed with Trump and his campaign manager, Corey Lewandowski, the possibility of arranging Trump's visit to Russia during the campaign as part of the Trump Tower negotiations.

According to Cohen, Trump told him to talk to Lewandowski and *'see what dates were available* for him to travel. Cohen further confessed that he briefed the president's children, Ivanka Trump, and Trump Jr., who were both serving the Trump Organization at the time as executives, approximately ten times about the Trump Tower deal. As he read 20 pages of his prepared testimony, Cohen also alleged that Trump frequently misrepresents his wealth to insurance companies, banks, and tax authorities to his advantage. Cohen further testified that he has more than 100 tapes of his clients and that Trump must have asked him to threaten entities or individuals more than 500 times over the past decade. Republicans lashed out at Cohen, stating that Trump's former lawyer is nothing but a liar.

They said he pleaded guilty to his crimes, including hush-money payments and multiple-year tax fraud, so why should anyone believe him now? Republicans said his anger and bitterness fueled Cohen's testimony for not getting a White House job. U.S. Representative and Republican Paul Gosar told Cohen,

"You're a pathological liar. You don't know truth from falsehood."

Cohen also went on and shared details about Stephanie Clifford's case. He said he conferred with the president about the payment several times just to make sure he was to pay or not. According to Cohen, Trump said, *"It's just $130,000. It's not a lot of money. And we should just do it. So go ahead and do it."*

Trump then directed Cohen and Weisselberg to figure out a safe way to arrange the payment to the porn star. Cohen revealed that Trump instructed him to use his funds in order *'to avoid any money being traced back to him that could negatively impact his campaign.'*

Cohen provided new details regarding his efforts to hide Trump's alleged involvement in the hush-money payments in 2018. Cohen said with help from Trump and Weisselberg; he crafted a statement he issued that said he used his funds to pay Clifford and WASN'T reimbursed by the Trump organization. Cohen said when Stephanie Clifford leaked the news of having sex with Trump, and The Wall Street Journal reported the non-disclosure agreement and monetary arrangement with Clifford's attorney back in January 2018, he purposefully didn't mention Trump's name in the statement because Trump had denied having a sexual encounter with the porn star. Cohen stated Trump wanted him to express that the president *'was not knowledgeable of these reimbursements, and he wasn't knowledgeable of my actions.'*

Cohen even shared his memory of visiting the Oval Office and Trump, while giving him a tour, saying to him, *"Don't worry, Michael. They were Fed-Exed from New York, and it takes a while for that to get through the White House system."* According to Cohen, Trump was referring to his reimbursement checks that he was to receive shortly.

The reimbursements to Cohen were labeled as legal fees by Weisselberg. However, federal prosecutors failed to find any monthly invoices that could connect to any legal services provided by Cohen at the time. After the 2016 election, Weisselberg authorized a payment to cover the related income taxes and added a $60,000 bonus.

Talking about the reimbursements, Cohen said before the committee, "I have fixed things, but I am no longer your 'fixer,' Mr. Trump."

During the presidential campaign, Cohen fixed another allegation made by former Playboy model Karen McDougal. She also claimed she had an affair with Trump. Of course, the president denied sexual encounters with both of these women.

Cohen then revealed information about WikiLeaks' plan to release Democratic emails during the 2016 campaign. Not only did he say Trump was aware of what was going to happen, but he also stated that Roger Stone, an informal adviser to Trump's campaign, had told Trump in a July 2016 phone call that, *"he had just gotten off the phone with Julian Assange and that...within a couple of days, there would be a massive dump of emails that would damage Hillary Clinton's campaign."*

Cohen even stated Trump's response to the news. He said Trump responded, "Wouldn't that be great?"

Michael Cohen shared financial statements from the years 2011 and 2012 that showed Trump's net worth to be between $4 billion and $5 billion. The 2013 statement further added $4 billion in brand value which brought the total to above $8 billion. Trump claimed during one of his presidential campaigns that he has a net worth exceeding $10 billion, whereas Bloomberg News estimated Trump's wealth at $2.84 billion.

Further on in his testimony, Cohen termed Trump as a racist who passed derogatory remarks about black people. According to Cohen, on occasion, Trump made a racist comment to him. Cohen said, *"He told me that black people would never vote for him because they were too stupid.* On another occasion, Cohen recalled, *"While we were once driving through a struggling neighborhood in Chicago, he commented that only black people could live that way."*

Moreover, Cohen showed the committee copies of a letter that he had sent on Trump's direct orders, threatening the president's high school, colleges, and the College Board not to release his SAT scores and grades.

The third testimony was on February 28, 2019, where Cohen testified behind closed doors to the

House Intelligence Committee for more than 7 hours.

Recently, Cohen wrote a public letter that recapped his extensive testimony before three congressional committees. The letter stated, *"Trump and his [White House] advisors encouraged Cohen to lie and say all Moscow Tower project contacts ended as of January 31, 2017, when the project was alive at least six months later."*

"Trump did so using 'code' language – telling Cohen during various conversations that there was 'no collusion, no Russian contacts, nothing about Russia' after the start of the campaign." The letter added.

CHAPTER FIFTEEN

— ◆ —

TRUMP 17

ON APRIL 18, 2019, a redacted copy of Special Counsel Robert Mueller's *"Report on the Investigation into Russian Interference in the 2016 Presidential Election,"* which is commonly known to the entire world as the Mueller Report, was released to the public. According to the report, which created ripples throughout America, there were two campaigns to elect the GOP candidate Donald Trump – Trump ran one campaign, and the Russian government ran another.

The said report objectively identified collusion between Russia and the Trump campaign. However, all such allegations were repeatedly denied by Trump and his senior advisers and close associates. Here are a few examples where members of the Trump team blatantly lied.

On July 24, 2016, Trump's Campaign Chairman Paul Manafort appeared on ABC's "This Week". When George Stephanopoulos asked him if there are any ties between Mr. Trump, you, or your campaign and Putin and his regime, Manafort responded, "No, there are not. That's absurd. And you know, there's no basis to it."

On July 27, 2016, Trump appeared on a CBS Miami news station. In response to allegations that Russia was trying to help him win the election, he told the host Jim DeFed, "I can tell you I think if I came up with that, they'd say, 'Oh, it's a conspiracy theory, it is ridiculous' ... I mean, I have nothing to do with Russia. I don't have any jobs in Russia. I'm all over the world, but we're not involved in Russia."

On February 16, 2017, Trump held a press conference and told reporters, "Russia is a ruse. I know you have to get up and ask a question. It's so important.

Russia is a ruse. I have nothing to do with Russia. Haven't made a phone call to Russia in years. Don't speak to people from Russia. Not that I wouldn't. I just have nobody to speak to. I spoke to Putin twice. He called me on the election. I told you this. And he called me at the inauguration, a few days ago. We had a very good talk, especially the second one, which lasted for a pretty long period of time. I'm sure you probably get it because it was classified. So I'm sure everybody in this room perhaps has it. But we had a very, very good talk. I have nothing to do with Russia. To the best of my knowledge, no person that I deal with does."

On February 19, 2017, White House Chief of Staff Reince Priebus went on "Fox News Sunday." When Wallace asked him whether the Trump team had any connections to Russia, Preibus said "No." Preibus went on to add, "Let me give you an example. First of all, The New York Times put out an article with no direct sources that said that the Trump campaign had constant contact with Russian spies, basically, you know, some treasonous type of accusations. We have now all kinds of people looking into this. I can assure you, and I have been approved to say this—that the top levels of the intelligence community have assured me that that story is not only inaccurate, but it's grossly overstated, and it was wrong. And there's nothing to it."

The report identified a total of 272 contacts between Trump's aides and operatives linked to Russia. These contacts also included at least 38 meetings (some of which were conducted on Skype). Also, there were at least 33 high-ranking officials and Trump advisers who were aware of contacts with Russia-linked operatives during the presidential campaign. The stated number also includes Trump himself. None of these contacts ever reported to the proper authorities. The Trump team did everything in its power to cover up every single one of them.

The Trump team went on and told many lies to the American people. Even Mueller himself repeatedly remarked on how far the Trump team was willing to go and cover up their contacts with their Russian contacts. Here's what Mueller stated:

"The investigation established that several individuals affiliated with the Trump Campaign lied to the Office, and to Congress, about their interactions with Russian-affiliated individuals and related matters. Those lies materially impaired the investigation of Russian election interference."

When Donald Trump signed a Letter of Intent addressed to a Russian developer for the Trump Tower Moscow deal, he proved his contact with Russians during the 2016 presidential campaign. Besides the reigning president of the United States, there were other members of the Trump team who had proven contacts with Russian during the said campaign.

The Associates That Maintained Close Ties with Russia

According to public statements, CNN reporting, court filings, and reporting from other news outlets, at least 16 associates of Donald Trump were said to have had contacts with Russians during the 2016 presidential campaign. The exchange of information, which was, at times, entirely confidential, was not always carried out utilizing face-to-face meetings. Besides personal sessions, these associates also engaged in telephonic conversations, emails, video chats, and emails. All of the following 16 associates never admitted to maintaining close ties or colluding with Russian operatives in the 2016 US elections.

1- Former Trump campaign chairman Paul Manafort tops the list of corrupt Trump associates. Manafort attended the June 2016 meeting held at Trump Tower with a group of Russians. These operatives were said to have dirt to throw on Democratic candidate Hillary Clinton. The next thing that went against Paul Manafort was his email and meeting with Konstantin Kilimnik, his Russian business associate, who, according to court records, is suspected of having ties with Russian intelligence.

2- **Senior Trump campaign official Rick Gates** was also involved in interactions held during the presidential campaign with Kilimnik. According to court records, based on those interactions, he was suspected of having ties to Russian intelligence, according to court records.

3- **Former national security adviser Michael Flynn** was the highlight throughout the entire Russia investigation. He exchanged text messages as well as phone calls with Russian ambassador Sergey Kislyak during the Trump transition. Also, he was reported to be with White House senior adviser and Trump's son-in-law Jared Kushner when they had a meeting with Kislyak in Trump Tower during the presidential campaign.

4- **Trump's son Donald Trump Jr.** attended the meeting at Trump Tower. Around that time, he also had three telephonic conversations with Emin Agalarov, the Russian pop star who helped him arrange the secret meeting. Trump Jr. was also briefly introduced to Alexander Torshin, a Russian banker, at a dinner during the National Rifle Association convention. According to what Federal prosecutors said in 2018, Torshin was the guy who handled the alleged Russian spy Maria Butina.

5- White House senior adviser, Jared Kushner, was another prominent figure who attended the secret meeting held at the Trump Tower during the presidential campaign back in 2016. He was also reported to have met Sergey Kislyak and Russian state banker Sergey Gorkov.

6- Trump campaign adviser George Papadopoulos had a meeting with Kremlin-connected professor Joseph Mifsud a few times. He also met with a suspicious Russian woman who claimed to be Vladimir Putin's niece. However, eventually, her claim was termed false. Papadopoulos was also in touch with Russian foreign policy analyst Ivan Timofeev.

7- Former Trump campaign adviser Carter Page had a meeting with Russian ambassador Sergey Kislyak during the Republican convention.

He also had a rendezvous with Russian lawmakers and an executive who was said to be from the Kremlin-controlled oil company called Rosneft. These meetings were conducted during his trips to Russia in July and December of 2016.

8- Former Attorney General Jeff Sessions met with Sergey Kislyak twice during the 2016 presidential campaign. The first meeting was arranged on the sidelines of the Republican convention, and the second meeting was in his Senate office in Washington in September of 2016.

9- Trump campaign official JD Gordon was another prominent figure who also met Sergey Kislyak during the Republican National Convention. According to Gordon himself, he spoke with the Russian ambassador at two separate events.

10- Former Trump campaign adviser Roger Stone met with a suspicious Russian guy back in May 2016. The shady guy called himself Henry Greenberg and offered dirt on Clinton in exchange for $2 million. Stone was also seen exchanging private Twitter messages with Russian intelligence operatives who were posing as the infamous hacker Guccifer 2.0.

11- Former Trump campaign aide Michael Caputo effortlessly played the role of a middleman. He was also in contact with the Russian man who went by Henry Greenberg. According to Caputo himself, he helped arrange Greenberg's meeting with former Trump campaign adviser Roger Stone.

12- Trump associate Erik Prince had a meeting with Russian state banker Kirill Dmitriev (head of the sanctioned Russian Direct Investment Fund) during a controversial January 2017 trip to Seychelles. According to what Prince told Congress, they met in Seychelles to discuss business.

13- White House official Avi Berkowitz, who served as Kushner's assistant, met with Kislyak during the Trump transition.

14- Former Trump attorney Michael Cohen kept in touch with at least two Russian companies during the 2016 US presidential campaign that showed interest in building a Trump Tower in Moscow. According to court filings, Cohen talked over the phone to someone from the office of Kremlin spokesman Dmitry Peskov for 20 minutes about the project. Also, Cohen spoke to an unknown Russian man who claimed to have influential connections in the political world. The same Russian guy offered *"political synergy"* with the Trump campaign.

15- White House senior adviser and Donald Trump's daughter Ivanka Trump was in touch with the wife of the Russian guy who offered *"political synergy"* to former Trump attorney Michael Cohen. According to Ivanka's spokesman, Trump's daughter received an email and passed it along to Michael Cohen.

16- Trump's business associate Felix Sater is a Russian-American real estate developer who previously worked with Trump on real estate deals. Throughout the Trump campaign, Sater was in contact with Russians as he worked with Michael Cohen to bring the Trump Tower Moscow to deal with fruition. Sater was acting as a broker between Michael Cohen and the Trump organization and various Russian individuals who were interested and involved in the project. Mueller's report included contacts where Sater operated as an intermediary and conveyed confidential information between the Russia-linked operatives and Trump.

17- White House communications director Anthony Scaramucci (The Mooch) had a meeting with Kirill Dmitriev at the 2017 Davos World Economic Forum. After the meeting, Scaramucci was seen criticizing U.S. sanctions on Russia in an interview he gave with a Russian news agency.

These 17 individuals in the Trump team were the ones who got the main attraction. Besides them, numerous other contacts surfaced throughout the Russia investigation that Mueller's report does not mention.

According to the Mueller report, *"around the time of the Presidential Inauguration,"* Paul Manafort had a meeting with Kilimnik and Ukrainian oligarch Serhiy Lyovochkin. Even though the exact date of this meeting cannot be determined, a footnote in the Mueller report states *"1/19/17 & 1/22/17 Kilimnik CBP Records"*. That is the same period that covers Trump's inauguration. Thus, it is not clear whether this contact took place during the campaign or after the inauguration. However, Mueller's report does not count this meeting as a contact. The Mueller report points out that Vladimir Putin directed numerous Russian people in business to get in touch with and maintain close contact with the Trump campaign team.

Petr Aven, a Russian oligarch and the head of Alfa Bank, took an interview Special Counsel's office an interview in which he discussed this topic. According to Aven, there were approximately 50 oligarchs who regularly met with Putin. He further said that he *"understood that any suggestions or critiques that Putin made during these meetings were implicit directives and that there would be consequences for him if he did not follow through."*

It is rather challenging to determine how many contacts occurred. For instance, the Papadopoulos indictment mentions at one point that he had 'several emails and skype exchanges' with Russians. However, in other situations, a conservative estimate of only two contacts is mentioned.

The Mueller report states, *"During the campaign period, Papadopoulos connected over LinkedIn with several MFA-affiliated individuals in addition to Timofeev. On April 25, 2016, he connected with Dmitry Andreyko, publicly identified as a First Secretary at the Russian Embassy in Ireland. In July 2016, he connected with Yuriy Melnik, the spokesperson for the Russian Embassy in Washington, and with Alexey Krasilnikov, publicly identified as a counselor with the MFA. And on September 16, 2016, he connected with Sergei Nalobin, also identified as an MFA official."*

The fact of the matter is that the Mueller report does not count the acts of connecting with an individual over LinkedIn as a contact unless there is evidence that proves the two parties exchanged an actual message. In Papadopoulos' case, his several messages to Sergei Millian, a Belarus-born businessman, over LinkedIn are considered contacts. However, if, in any future investigations, it indicated that Papadopoulos exchanged personalized messages when connecting (or after connecting) with any of the individuals as mentioned earlier, these connections will be counted as contacts.

CHAPTER SIXTEEN

— ◇ —

INVESTIGATIONS & MYSTERY INFORMATION(S) FOUND AND PROVIDED TO CHIEF OF JUSTICE JOHN

IN NOVEMBER LAST YEAR (2017), the Trump administration announced a new policy that required migrants to apply for asylum only at legal border crossings. Currently, migrants enter the United States illegally and then seek asylum. Judge Jon Tigar of the U.S. District Court for the Northern District of California went ahead and issued a temporary restraining order. That blocked the new policy from going into effect. That is what Tigar declared:

"The president may not rewrite the immigration laws to impose a condition that Congress has expressly forbidden."

This enraged Trump who didn't wait for long and stated while talking to reporters. The president criticized Tigar by calling him *"an Obama judge."* The taunt directed to the fact that it was Obama who appointed him back in 2012. That's not where Trump stopped. He went on and called the Ninth Circuit Court, where Northern District cases appealed *"a disgrace."*

"Every case gets filed in the Ninth Circuit because they know that's not law. That's not what this country stands for. Every case that gets filed in the Ninth Circuit, we get beaten ... People should not be allowed to immediately run to this very friendly circuit and file their case." The President further said, *"we will win [the asylum case] in the Supreme Court of the United States."*

Trump's comments and insults were too much for the ordinarily reticent Chief Justice John Roberts to abide by. In response, Roberts didn't delay his statement to the Associated Press. He said, *"We do not have Obama judges or Trump judges, Bush judges or Clinton judges. What we have is an extraordinary group of dedicated judges doing their level best to do equal rights to those appearing before them. The independent judiciary is something we should all be thankful for."*

Following Roberts' statement, a verbal fight ensued between him and President Trump. Trump took to Twitter and said, *"Sorry Chief Justice Roberts, but you do indeed have Obama judges, and they have a much different point of view than the people who are charged with the safety of our country."*

Trump even went on to deny that the Ninth Circuit represented *"an independent judiciary".*

Chief Justice Roberts Intervened in Special Counsel Robert Mueller's Investigations

In 2018, the Supreme Court jumped right in to intervene in the operations of Special Counsel Robert Mueller's investigation. At first, not much was known as to what was going on beyond the mechanics of an order issued by Chief Justice John Roberts.

Here is what the order issued by the Chief Justice of the United States stated: *"It is ordered that the order of the United States District Court for the District of Columbia holding the applicant in contempt, including the accrual of monetary penalties, is hereby stayed pending receipt of a response, due on or before Monday, December 31, 2018, by noon, and further order of the undersigned or the Court."*

The order left the underlying issue entirely opaque. Here's what Kevin Daley of the Daily Caller News Foundation put together based on the minimal evidence that was available at the time about the matter:

"Very little is known of the case, because the matter has proceeded through the federal courts under seal, meaning strict confidentiality prevails over every detail.

The scant facts which are available about the case are these: a grand jury issued a subpoena to an unnamed company owned by a foreign government sometime during the summer of 2018. That firm, referred to in court filings as "the corporation" has been fighting the subpoena in federal court since August.

The U.S. Court of Appeals for the D.C. Circuit released one of the matters on December 18. Since the entity is owned by a foreign government, it sought to quash the subpoena under the protections of the Foreign Sovereign Immunities Act. The D.C. Circuit rejected those arguments and found that the corporation must comply with the subpoena.

The company appealed that decision to the Supreme Court. The corporation faces a fine for every day that it fails to abide by the subpoena."

Was Mystery Subpoena Clash Tied to Mueller's Investigations?

Supreme Court Chief Justice John Roberts weighed in on a clash over a mysterious grand jury subpoena, which was rumored to connect to Special Counsel Robert Mueller's investigation. It revealed that the dispute involved an unknown company owned by a foreign country, which fought the subpoena and later appealed a related contempt citation.

The Chief Justice stayed the contempt citation and all the associated financial penalties that were pending as a response from government lawyers. The crux of the clash between the mysterious company and prosecutors remains clear even to this date. However, according to Politico, the dispute seemed to involve Mueller's team.

In October 2018, a Politico reporter overheard a man (connected to the appeal) request a copy of the special counsel's latest filing in the case while sitting in the D.C. Circuit Court of Appeals clerk's office.[1] The man declined to identify himself or his client. In December 2018, when the case was heard, the public and journalists were not allowed inside the courtroom. All the journalists were reportedly ordered to leave the floor where lawyers were presenting their positions. It reported that an entire floor of the D.C. federal courthouse was locked down by security in the morning; the company's appeal argument was scheduled. Strict security measures were taken to ensure privacy. The lawyers entering and leaving the courtroom were not to be seen.

The scant information the public about the case revealed that a three-judge D.C. Circuit panel that examined the appeal rejected the company's argument that it is immune from grand jury subpoenas under the Foreign Sovereign Immunities Act (FISA), and that complying with the same would be violating the law in the corporation's home country.

Later, a discussion ensued that whether or not Mueller's team was involved in the case. When asked directly, Mueller's team did not make any public comments regarding the dispute. The curiosity about the ongoing conflict rose suspicion that the president's office was involved in the case. The lawyers for President Trump told The New York Times that the evidence does not include the president. They said they were not even aware of the nature of this litigation.

"We're not involved in it — we're not aware of the nature or scope of the litigation," Jay Sekulow, one of the president's lawyers, told The New York Times.

There were speculations everywhere. Everyone was trying to get to the bottom of this case whose nature was kept a secret from the public and journalists. Minimal information leaked regarding the case and the identity of the foreign country to which the unknown company belonged, was also kept under wraps. The case was under seal, and strict confidentiality prevailed. As of now, the company faces penalties fined daily until they comply with the subpoena.

The Government Filed a Sealed Response to Supreme Court

When Chief Justice John Roberts issued a temporary pause on an order holding an unnamed foreign government-owned company in contempt over a mystery court case that was seemingly related to special counsel Robert Mueller's investigation, the federal government issued its response that was filed under seal. For those who don't know, this is the first publicly known legal challenge seemingly related to Mueller's investigation that has made its way to the Supreme Court. The Chief Justice's original order put on hold the contempt citation issued by a D.C. federal judge against the company because it repeatedly refused to comply with a grand jury subpoena. It was then the justices decided if they wanted to intervene in the case or not.

The company asked the Supreme Court to intervene after a federal appeals court ruling. According to the verdict, the company was ordered to comply with the subpoena. Should the company choose to comply with the subpoena, it would have to turn over information, even confidential information, of its commercial activity in a criminal investigation led by special counsel Robert Mueller. The Supreme Court's action also paused all the fines the company in question was facing for every single day it spent in noncompliance with the subpoena.

The company began challenging the subpoena in September 2018. In its ruling, the U.S. Circuit Court of Appeals for the District of Columbia put forward a few clues about the company and its country of origin. The clues also hinted why Mueller's team was after the company.

As far as the identity of the company is concerned, there's a vast range of possibilities to consider. According to the speculations in the public, the company could be anything from a sovereign-owned bank to a state-backed technology or information company. Corporate entities along the same lines have been frequent recipients of requests for information in Mueller's investigation.

Although the prime focus of the Mueller team was to investigate the ties between the Trump campaign and Russia's efforts to interfere in the 2016 presidential election, prosecutors revealed that the Mueller team was also looking into the suspicious activities related to Ukrainian, Turkish, and other foreign government interests.

The company in the Supreme Court challenge and the grand jury proceeding related to it have stayed a secret to this date. To everyone's surprise, prosecutors, the company in question, and the circuit court took extreme pains to keep the identities of every entity involved in the case shrouded in layers of secrecy.

The Role of Judge Greg Kansas

On September 7, 2017, President Trump decided against nominating Katsas to serve as a United States Circuit Judge of the United States Court of Appeals for the District of Columbia Circuit. He filled the seat vacated by Judge Janice Rogers Brown, who retired at the end of August 2017. Interestingly, in 2017, Katsas recused himself from any cases related to Mueller's investigation on which he had personally worked while serving in the White House during the Trump administration. Needless to mention, Katsas also recused himself from the subpoena case.

That was another clue that connected the incident to Mueller because D.C. Circuit Judge Greg Katsas was the only one of the court's 10 active judges to recuse himself from the matter. He was also the sole judge in the court appointed by Trump and had worked on the Russia investigation.

The Company's Debatable Country of Origin

Because of everything that has been reported about Mueller's report so far, there appear to be two strong possibilities regarding the company's country of origin.

The first possibility is that the company is Russian. For obvious reasons, this could be a state-owned Russian company. The Steele dossier made uncorroborated claims about the planned payoffs to Trump associates that involved the oil company, Rosneft. That could be a possibility because Erik Prince, Trump's transition adviser, met the manager of a Russian sovereign wealth fund in Seychelles. There have been other claims according to which the bank VTB was involved in the Trump Tower Moscow talks. It also reported that the chair of a different bank, VEB, met with Jared Kushner during the campaign.

The second possibility is that the company could be a Gulf state company. Many reports have cleared that Mueller was scrutinizing money trails and influence operations from the Gulf States. United Arab Emirates, Saudi Arabia, and Qatar were said to have come under Mueller's scrutiny.

The level of secrecy and mystery involved in this case has piqued the interest of numerous journalists but to no avail. That's because the details of the subpoena case are well-guarded to this date.

CHAPTER SEVENTEEN

— • —

THE ATTORNEY GEN. BARR REPORT VS. THE SECRET MUELLER REPORT VS. THE REASONABLE DOUBT

U.S. ATTORNEY GENERAL WILLIAM Barr released a letter that he said was a summarized version of Mueller's report that he received from Special Counsel Robert Mueller about the alleged crimes that President Trump was said to have committed. General Barr condensed the over 400-page Mueller report into just four pages.

In his letter to Congress, Attorney General Barr wrote that the president's exoneration is complete concerning any conspiracy between Russian intelligence and the Trump campaign. He further stated that there was no collusion between Trump's team and Russian intelligence in the 2016 presidential election. Barr also wrote that although Trump will not be prosecuted by the Department of Justice for obstruction of justice, the special counsel did not exonerate him.

Now, this turns out to be a head-scratcher. Why did Barr reveal any uncertainty on the part of anyone in the Department of Justice when he shouldn't have? Also, under the Federal Rules of Criminal Procedure, he should not have done that. Those rules, which strictly prohibit the revelation of evidence for and against the prosecution of people not prosecuted, also prohibit the revelation of the existence of such evidence and any disagreements among prosecutors over the legal significance of the evidence.

The disclosure that Barr made is tantamount to the same violation of federal rules and Department of Justice policy that FBI Director James Comey committed when he declared in the summer of 2016 that Hillary Clinton would not be prosecuted for using private servers to exchange classified information and then later revealed that the FBI had convincing evidence against her. He later went on to explain what that evidence was.

When Trump learned about the Barr summary of the Mueller report, he ended up rejoicing. Then without thinking through his idea and consulting his lawyers, he asked for the Mueller report to be made public. That was a huge mistake.

Barr's Four-Page Summary

Barr's four-page summary of Mueller's report was based on Mueller's principal conclusions. A careful reading of it reveals the lawyerly language that Trump does not want to hear. Although the president will not be charged with conspiracy to obtain something of value from the Russians to affect the presidential campaign, which is a felony, it is clear that Mueller found some evidence of a conspiracy between Russian intelligence and the Trump campaign. That evidence was the communications carried out between them, some in person and some over Skype or telephone.

However, according to the summary, the evidence that Mueller found was not sufficient enough to prove the existence of the conspiracy beyond a reasonable doubt. Of course, Mueller found some evidence of such conspiracy because had he failed to find any evidence, Barr would have highlighted the fact in his summary, which he didn't.

The second conclusion derived from Barr's summary of the Mueller report is that Mueller found the evidence against Trump of interfering or attempting to interfere, with an FBI investigation for a self-serving purpose to be equivocal. Meaning, whatever evidence that Mueller found was as strong as exculpatory evidence that builds a valid case for not prosecuting him. In the conspiracy charge, Mueller concluded that he could not prove the case beyond a reasonable doubt. On the obstruction charge, Mueller allowed his boss, Attorney General Barr, to decide whether or not the president should be prosecuted. Why Barr revealed, all this information remains a mystery because it forced the release of Mueller's full report, and also the evidence on which the said report was based so that members of Congress can examine for themselves what evidence of obstruction and conspiracy did Mueller find.

Releasing Mueller's full report is easier said than done. That's because the report itself is a summary of millions of pages of hard evidence that Mueller and his team accumulated. That hard evidence includes grand jury transcripts, transcripts of wiretaps, FBI notes of interrogations of witnesses, emails and text messages, prosecutors' impressions of the quality of their evidence; and more than 1 million pages of campaign and White House documents voluntarily surrendered to Mueller. If the almost 450-page report, on which Barr's summary is based, was to be released in its entirety, everyone knew there would be much in there for Trump's adversaries to feast upon.

The Mueller Report Was More Damaging Than Barr Revealed

According to The New York Times report, some of Mueller's investigators told associates that William Barr did not do justice to the findings of their inquiry and did adequately portray them. They said the findings were more trouble for President Trump than Barr made them sound in his concise summary.

Attorney General Barr stated that he would soon release the lengthy report for public viewing, but he would need time to scrub out all the confidential and sensitive information, like classified material, secret grand-jury testimony, and information related to current federal investigations. Barr said he had identified four categories based on which he will redact information from the report when it gets released to the public. Those four categories were:

- Grand-jury material

- Classified information

- Information connected to pending investigations

- Information that would invade the privacy of peripheral third parties

The special counsel's investigators had written multiple summaries of the report. Thus, some believed that Barr should have included more information about their material in the four-page letter that he wrote to Congress, focusing only on the main conclusions. The investigators claimed Barr cited the special counsel's work only briefly in his letter, which is why it did not present an accurate and fair view of the matter under investigation.

Even though the report is said to examine the president's efforts to thwart the investigation by Mueller's team, the officials interviewed refused to shed light on as to why some of the special counsel's investigators thought their findings were potentially more damaging for Trump than William Barr explained in his summary.

The attorney general refrained from revealing the details of the investigation led by the special counsel team. In the letter sent to Congress, Barr identified federal rule 6(e) that restricted him from revealing certain grand jury information.

Attorney General William Barr and his advisers expressed their frustrations about Mueller and his team, which included 19 lawyers, about 40 FBI agents, and other personnel. According to two government officials, Barr and other Justice Department officials thought that the special counsel's investigators could not uphold their task when they failed to decide whether or not Trump illegally obstructed the inquiry. When Mueller could not make any judgment on the obstruction matter, Barr made his own decision. He stepped in to declare that he had cleared Trump of wrongdoing.

Barr clearing Trump of wrongdoing is, as a matter of fact, based on the Mueller report, which states that none of Trump's campaign members conspired or coordinated with the Russian government. The report further says that Russian intelligence tried to influence the elections through the Internet Research Agency (IRA) and hacking into Hillary Clinton's email server.

Barr said Mueller found no conspiracy between Trump's campaign and the Russian government during the 2016 presidential election. Barr wrote: *"Mueller decided to skip a prosecutorial judgment, so that leaves it to the attorney general to determine whether the conduct described in the report constitutes a crime."* He and his deputy, Rod J. Rosenstein, finally decided that the evidence was insufficient to conclude that the president had committed an obstruction offense.

However, William Barr cautioned that Mueller's report states that *"while this report does not conclude that the president committed a crime, it also does not exonerate him"* on the obstruction of justice issue.

Barr came under criticism for sharing so little from the Mueller report. However, the officials that are familiar with the Attorney General's way of working and thinking said he and his aides limited the details because they were worried about wading into the political territory. Barr and his advisers told if they had included derogatory information about Trump while clearing him, they would have faced a storm of criticism similar to what James Comey had to endure in the Clinton investigation.

Making the Mueller Report Public

Mueller, in his investigation, examined Trump's attempts to maintain control over the research. His efforts included his firing of James Comey and ousting Mueller and Attorney General Jeff Sessions to install a loyalist to oversee the inquiry. However, Barr's letter that outlined only the main findings of the investigation overshadowed his longstanding intent to make public as much of the entire report as possible. It was his goal since his confirmation hearing.

He said to lawmakers that he wanted the public and Congress to read the report. He further said the department would furnish a version of the report by mid-April 2019 with all the sensitive material redacted and present it to Congress. He also offered to testify on Capitol Hill soon after turning over the report. Under the relevant regulations, Barr can publicly release as much of the Mueller report as he deems appropriate.

William Barr and Robert Mueller have been friends for the last 30 years. Barr said during his confirmation hearing that he trusted Mueller to lead an impartial investigation. He said he told the president that Mueller was a *straight shooter who should be dealt with as such.* Mueller served as the head of the Justice Department's criminal division when Barr was attorney general under George Bush. Their families happen to be friends. The promises Barr made of transparency have done little to appease Democrats. As a result, the House Judiciary Committee voted to let its chairman use a subpoena to compel Attorney General William Barr to hand over a full copy of the Mueller report and all the underlying evidence to Congress. The chairman, Representative Jerrold Nadler, Democrat of New York, did not confirm at the time when exactly he would use a subpoena. However, he made it clear that he did not trust Barr's characterization of what Mueller and his team found in the investigation. Here is what he said:

"The Constitution charges Congress for withholding the president accountable for alleged official misconduct. That job requires us to evaluate the evidence for ourselves — not the attorney general's summary, not a substantially redacted synopsis, but the full report and the underlying evidence."

Republicans have rejoiced and cheered over William Barr's letter that cleared Trump. They went on to accuse Democrats of trying to prolong the cloud over Donald Trump's presidency and urged them to move on instead of targeting him. The president himself has embraced Barr's version of events. He pronounced the outcome of the investigation a *"complete and total exoneration."* He called for the Justice Department and his allies on Capitol Hill to investigate and hold accountable all those who were responsible for opening an inquiry against him.

Democrats Ready Challenge Barr's Letter and Fight for Mueller's Complete Findings

House Democrats were anxious and expressed their concern that President Trump's attorney general may be withholding evidence of wrongdoing that was uncovered by special counsel Robert S. Mueller and his team. As soon as Barr's letter surfaced in the political arena, Democrats started preparing for potential battles to acquire access to the full contents of Mueller's report. They vowed to pursue the acquisition and any underlying investigative materials in court if necessary.

"We will fight for the full report," Representative Jerrold Nadler, Democrat of New York and chairman of the House Judiciary Committee, said.

He emphasized that Democrats have the full right to expect complete transparency from Mueller and the Justice Department, except for redactions of classified information that could potentially jeopardize sensitive law enforcement methods if disclosed publicly. On the other hand, Attorney General William Barr noted that neither he nor his predecessors ever challenged any actions that Mueller took during his nearly two-year-long probe into the matter. However, with limited power to force information out of potential witnesses, congressional Democrats are looking forward to Mueller's complete findings to inform them of Trump's campaign, businesses, and alleged foreign ties. They have explicitly stated that they will not be satisfied with anything less than a complete account of the results and the evidence that helped form the report.

"The Special Counsel's investigation focused on questions that go to the integrity of our democracy itself: whether foreign powers corruptly interfered in

our elections, and whether unlawful means were used to hinder that investigation," House Speaker Nancy Pelosi, Democrat of California and Senate Minority Leader Charles E. Schumer, Democrat of New York said in a joint statement after Attorney General William Barr announced Special Counsel Robert Mueller had completed his report. "The American people have a right to the truth. The watchword is transparency."

The stakes were high at the time. Everyone believed that if the special counsel found evidence that Trump committed a crime, participated in a coverup, or engaged in conduct undermining the public trust, it would fuel calls for impeachment. According to the Justice Department, Mueller did not recommend any further indictments. It was news that Trump's defenders in the GOP took as vindication.

"The reports that there will be no new indictments confirm what we've known all along: there was never any collusion with Russia," Representative Steve

Scalise, Republican of Los Angeles and the House's second-ranking Republican, said in a statement.

However, Democrats were not ready to lay down their weapons and believe that truth was not being withheld from the public. Trump's disdain for Mueller's investigation, which he blatantly labeled a witch hunt and considered presidential harassment, had fed Democrats' suspicion that the president might have something to hide and might attempt to force Attorney General William Barr to conceal any unpleasant details from public view.

Consequently, Pelosi and Schumer warned that it was imperative for Barr to publicize Mueller's complete findings no later than President Trump was made aware of the report's contents. They said, *"Attorney General Barr must not give President Trump, his lawyers, or his staff any 'sneak preview' of Special Counsel Mueller's findings or evidence. The White House must not be allowed to interfere in decisions about what parts of those findings or evidence are made public."*

Republicans were also in favor of releasing the full report. However, they stopped echoing the Democrats' concerns and expressed faith that William Barr will be as transparent as possible. This indicated they would defer to Barr, not fight him.

"We're jumping about 60 steps too far." The Judiciary Committee's ranking minority-party member, Representative Douglas A. Collins, Republican of Georgia said when asked about Democrats' plans. "At this point in time, I'm not going to question my attorney general's veracity or the fact that he's going to do what he says he's going to do. Until he proves me wrong."

— · —

THE COVER-UP IN ORDER TO CLEAR THE PRESIDENT

THE FACT THAT ATTORNEY General William Barr had truncated quotes and omitted key context in his summary of special counsel Robert Mueller's report was proven when the special counsel's report was released in April 2019.

William Barr Twisted the Language and Tone of the Mueller's Report

In his letter, Barr clipped the first half of a sentence that substantially changed the entire tone of Mueller's findings on whether Trump's team colluded with Russians in the 2016 US presidential election. Mueller had based his finding pertaining to collusion on an unflattering point:

"Although the investigation established that the Russian government perceived it would benefit from a Trump presidency and worked to secure that outcome and that the Campaign expected it would benefit electorally from information stolen and released through Russian efforts, the investigation did not establish that members of the Trump Campaign conspired or coordinated with the Russian government in its election interference activities."

However, in his summarized letter, Barr only used the second half of the statement, i.e. *"The investigation did not establish that members of the Trump campaign conspired or coordinated with the Russian government in its election interference activities."*

This edit made a striking difference. It made the Trump campaign look not at fault and better than Mueller's full statement did. The abovementioned discrepancy was highlighted by the press and was widely discussed on social media. Barr's critics took to Twitter and said this was an *'example of how the attorney general sought to spin the investigation's findings in his boss's favor.'*

Similarly, Barr also misrepresented Mueller's approach to the question of collusion. In one of his press conferences, Barr confidently said that Mueller found 'no collusion,' 'no underlying collusion,' and 'no evidence of collusion.' Here's what he exactly said:

"There was no evidence of the Trump campaign's collusion with the Russian government's hacking." Barr further added, "There was, in fact, no collusion."

However, the very beginning of Mueller's report makes it clear that the special counsel did not evaluate if there was collusion. That's because collusion is not a federal crime or a commonly used legal term. Instead, the report was more focused on evaluating whether there was a conspiracy or a criminal act, or coordination between the Trump campaign and Russian intelligence. Nonetheless, the report did state that the investigation did not find evidence to establish coordination. The passage in the report reads:

In evaluating whether evidence about the collective action of multiple individuals constituted a crime, we applied the framework of conspiracy law, not the concept of "collusion." In so doing, the Office recognized that the word "collude" was used in communications with the Acting Attorney General confirming certain aspects of the investigation's scope and that the term has frequently been invoked in public reporting about the investigation. But collusion is not a specific offense or theory of liability found in the United States Code, nor is it a term of art in federal criminal law. For those reasons, the Office's focus in analyzing questions of joint criminal liability was on conspiracy as defined in federal law.

In another instance, Barr's language and tone on obstruction do not properly capture Mueller's determination on the issue. Mueller, in his report, wrote: *"If we had confidence after a thorough investigation of the facts that the President clearly did not commit obstruction of justice, we would so state. Based on the facts and the applicable legal standards, however, we are unable to reach that judgment."*

On the other hand, Barr told the public that Mueller was neutral on the said matter: *"The Special Counsel, therefore, did not draw a conclusion — one way or the other — as to whether the examined conduct constituted obstruction."*

In his controversial letter to Congress, Barr also shaded the president's cooperation in Mueller's probe in a more favorable light than Mueller. Barr wrote: *"The White House fully cooperated with the special counsel's investigation, providing unfettered access to campaign and White House documents, directing senior aides to testify freely and asserting no privilege claims. At the same time, the president took no action that, in fact, deprived the special counsel of the documents and witnesses necessary to complete his investigation."*

According to Mueller, Trump himself refrained from cooperating. He wrote in his report: *"We also sought a voluntary interview with the President. After more discussion, the President declined to be interviewed."*

The report also implicated that Trump pressured a witness, Trump's former national security adviser, Michael Flynn. The report says, *"When Flynn's counsel reiterated that Flynn could no longer share information pursuant to a joint defense agreement, the President's personal counsel said he would make sure that the President knew that Flynn's actions reflected 'hostility' towards the President."*

It turns out that Attorney General William Barr's summary of Robert Mueller's findings didn't just tighten up the findings. They misrepresented the key points.

Barr Has a History of Writing Summaries That Obscure the Truth

It turns out that William Barr is infamous for writing summaries that withhold the truth from the public. *According to The Washington Post, Ryan Goodman, a New York University professor of law and former Defense Department special counsel, detailed a remarkably similar fight from 1989 in which Barr, then head of the Justice Department's Office of Legal Counsel, was involved. The Office of Legal Counsel had determined that the FBI was allowed to take people into custody in foreign countries without the consent of those countries' governments — a ruling that seemed to pave the way for the eventual arrest of former Panamanian leader Manuel Antonio Noriega.*

This was a contentious position to take, and Barr was asked to provide the memo offering the detailed legal rationale for allowing such detentions. He declined, instead offering a 13-page document that "summarizes the principal conclusions." When Congress, and then The Washington Post, obtained the full opinion in 1991, it was quickly noted that several conclusions from the full document hadn't been included in Barr's summary. Foremost among them was that the opinion authorized the president of the United States to ignore the United Nations Charter.

Goodman quoted what professor Jeanne Woods wrote in a 1996 Boston University law journal: *"Barr's congressional testimony attempted to gloss over the broad legal and policy changes that his written opinion advocated."*

Goodman further told The Washington Post that *"the 1989 situation "breeds a lot of distrust of relying on Barr's assurances that he's handling this process in a way that's faithful to the principles that he's announced and will let the public know what the public should know."*

When asked if he believed Barr acted in good faith back in 1989, Goodman said, *"I think it's difficult to imagine that Barr didn't know what he was doing in failing to inform the Congress that he had concluded that the president of the United States could violate the U.N. Charter. In fact, that proposition has proved to be highly controversial ever since the 'Office of Legal Counsel' opinion was publicly released, and significant executive branch practice turns on that proposition."*

Mueller's Response to Barr's Summary of His Report

Robert Mueller spoke in his defense and objected to William Barr's characterization of the findings of the Russia investigation and requested the attorney general to release the summaries of the report prepared by the special counsel. Attempting to disregard the summary on the basis of which Trump claimed total exoneration, Mueller said, *"Barr's summary of the investigation's principal conclusions 'did not fully capture the context, nature, and substance' of the probe."*

He further said, *"There is now a public confusion about critical aspects of the results of our investigation. This threatens to undermine a central purpose for which the Department appointed the Special Counsel: to assure full public confidence in the outcome of the investigations."*

In response, Barr went on to defend his summary that disclosed Mueller's bottom-line conclusions. Here's what he said:

"My main focus was the prompt release of a public version of the report so that Congress and the American people could read it for themselves and draw their own conclusions. The department's principal responsibility in conducting this investigation was to determine whether the conduct reviewed constituted a crime that the department could prove beyond a reasonable doubt. As attorney general, I serve as the chief law-enforcement officer of the United States, and it is my responsibility to ensure that the department carries out its law-enforcement functions appropriately. The special counsel's investigation was no exception."

The Trump Cover-up

Once the Mueller report got released, Democrats began vocalizing their idea of impeaching Trump on account of colluding with the Russian government. Amidst all this tension, a new talking point emerged: President Trump is involved in a cover-up.

House Speaker Nancy Pelosi, a Democrat of California, *"We do believe that it's important to follow the facts. We believe that no one is above the law, including the president of the United States. And we believe that the president of the United States is engaged in a cover-up."*

MSNBC's Andrea Mitchell shed light on how the president is engaged in the cover-up by not turning over documents (including his tax returns), letting aides testify before Congress, and asserting executive privilege on the Mueller report.

Of course, Donald Trump denied this charge.

"Instead of walking in happily into a meeting, I walk in to look at people that have just said that I was doing a cover-up". "I don't do cover-ups."

The president blasted the so-called phony investigations and Democratic calls for his impeachment. In a surprise White House press conference, Trump said, *"This whole thing was a take-down attempt at the president of the United States."* He was referring to special counsel Robert Mueller's investigation of Russian interference in the 2016 presidential election, possible collusion by members of the Trump campaign, and possible obstruction of justice by Trump himself.

In his final report, Robert Mueller said that Russian agents tried to influence the outcome of the 2016 election to benefit Trump. However, he did not find evidence that members of Trump's campaign coordinated with Russians in that effort. Mueller also said that he *"found multiple acts by the President"* that could have exercised *"undue influence"* over law enforcement investigations, including the Russia probe. Despite all of that, he did not conclude whether Trump had obstructed justice.

Trump went on to say, *"The media should be ashamed of themselves for how they have reported on Mueller's investigation. Here's the bottom line: There was no collusion; there was no obstruction. The crime was committed on the other side. I don't speak to Russians about campaigns. It's a hoax. The greatest hoax in history."*

Trump, in his press conference, said, *"If someday a Democrat becomes president and you have a Republican House, they can impeach him for any reason, or her, any reason. We can't allow that to happen. We can't allow it to happen."*

In the press conference, when the president was asked if he respected Congress as a co-equal branch of government with rights to oversight over the executive branch, Trump replied, *"I respect the courts. I respect Congress. I respect right here where we're standing. But what they have done is abuse. This is investigation Number 4 on the same thing. Probably five. And it really started I think pretty much from the time we came down the escalator in Trump Tower."*

Trump was referring to the launch of his campaign for the White House in 2015. He further said, *"We're doing a lot without them. Let them play their games. We're going to go down one track at a time. Let them finish up, and we'll be all set."*

Citing the cost of the Mueller investigation, Trump went on to say, *"These are the people that after two years and $40 million or $35 million, it will end up being a lot more than that by the time all of it is done. This is what happened."*

"No collusion. No obstruction. No nothing. They issued 50 orders authorizing the use of pen registers. Think of that — 500 witnesses. And then I have Nancy Pelosi go out and say that the president of the United States engaged in a cover-up. Now, we've had a House investigation.

We have Senate investigations. We have investigations like nobody has ever had, and we did nothing wrong. They would have loved to have said we colluded. They would have loved it. These people were out to get us. The Republican Party and President

Trump. They were out to get us. This was a one-sided horrible thing."

William Barr Helped Cover up the President's Biggest Crime

The entire world struggled to digest the enormity of Attorney General William Barr's corruption – how he tried to withhold the truth from the public. Now that Robert Mueller's redacted report has been released, here's what people must know:

- Russia launched a *"sweeping and systematic"* attack on the American political system, which undermined the integrity of American presidential elections, to elect Donald Trump as president.

- U.S. law enforcement launched an investigation that was aimed at getting to the bottom of that attack so that they could understand what exactly happened in order to ensure the integrity of future presidential elections.

- Donald Trump attempted in multiple ways to derail the accounting of this massive attack on the American political system and then tried to bury the truth in a manner that was at best corrupt, and at worst criminal.

Barr, hi, quoted that the Mueller report claimed Mueller had not established criminal conspiracy. However, Barr omitted the sentence that said the Trump campaign *"expected"* to *"benefit"* from Russian help. Barr also took Mueller's words to omit the conclusion that Trump was motivated to obstruct the investigation because it *"would call into question the legitimacy of his election"* by spotlighting Russian interference.

With Barr's summary, Trump claimed total exoneration. It obscured Trump and his campaign's embrace of Russian interference and the president's extensive efforts to prevent an accounting of it. Mueller has concluded there was *"substantial evidence"* to prove that Trump had acted with corrupt intent *"to deflect or prevent further scrutiny."*

However, Barr went on to claim that Trump shouldn't have been indicted. He argued that the president's *underlying misconduct itself* was no big deal. Barr also that Trump had the power to terminate the investigation if he believed he was being *"falsely accused,"* and it wouldn't display *"corrupt intent."* His statement actually put Trump above the law and cleared Trump of the *underlying misconduct* – his efforts to mislead Mueller's investigation into a Russian attack on the 2016 presidential election. Barr stated the president's misconduct was no big thing because he had been forced to be a part of that investigation. Barr's continuous efforts to understate the importance of Mueller's investigation itself cannot be ignored. His attempts lead us to the replacement narrative.

The way he twisted the report indicates that the probe was illegitimately aimed at removing Trump and that investigators corruptly let go of the real criminal, i.e., Hillary Clinton. In all honesty, the idea that there was no legal basis for the investigation is another way of saying that the Russian attack on the American political system. Regardless of any criminal conspiracy associated with it, was not worth investigating, and Trump's collusion with Russian intelligence is also no big deal.

At the hearing, Barr even shared his idea that Hillary Clinton may have been the real colluder. He and the Trump team's embrace of Russian help made a difference in the outcome of the 2016 presidential election.

Chapter Nineteen

Mueller Report Exposed

THE OPENING STATEMENT OF Robert Mueller's testimony to Congress on July 24, 2019, deserves the attention of every American:

"Good morning, Chairman Nadler, Ranking Member Collins, and members of the Committee.

As you know, in May 2017, the Acting Attorney General asked me to serve as Special Counsel. I undertook that role because I believed that it was of paramount interest to the nation to determine whether a foreign adversary had interfered in the presidential election.

As the Acting Attorney General said at the time, the appointment was 'necessary for the American people to have full confidence in the outcome.' My staff and I carried out this assignment with that critical objective in mind: to work quietly, thoroughly, and with integrity so that the public would have full confidence in the outcome. The order appointing me as Special Counsel directed our Office to investigate Russian interference in the 2016 presidential election. This included investigating any links or coordination between the Russian government and individuals associated with the Trump campaign. It also included investigating efforts to interfere with or obstruct the investigation. Throughout the investigation, I continually stressed two things to the team that we had assembled.

First, we needed to do our work as thoroughly as possible and as expeditiously as possible. It was in the public interest for our investigation to be complete, but not to last a day longer than necessary.

Second, the investigation needed to be conducted fairly and with absolute integrity. Our team would not leak or take other actions that could compromise the integrity of our work. All decisions were made based on the facts and the law. During our investigation, we charged more than 30 defendants with committing federal crimes, including 12 officers of the Russian military. Seven defendants have been convicted or pled guilty. Certain of the charges we brought remain pending today. For those matters, I stress that the indictments contain allegations, and every defendant is presumed innocent unless and until proven guilty. In addition to the criminal charges we brought, as required by Justice Department regulations, we submitted a confidential report to the Attorney General after the investigation. The report set forth the results of our work and the reasons for our charging and declination decisions. The Attorney General later made the report largely public. As you know, I made a few limited remarks about our report when we closed the Special Counsel's Office in May of this year.

Third, our investigation of efforts to obstruct the investigation and lie to investigators was of critical importance. Obstruction of justice strikes at the core of the government's effort to find the truth and hold wrongdoers accountable.

Finally, as described in Volume 2 of our report, we investigated a series of actions by the President towards the investigation. Based on Justice Department policy and principles of fairness, we decided we would not make a determination as to whether the President committed a crime. That was our decision then, and it remains our decision today.

Let me say a further word about my appearance today. It is unusual for a prosecutor to testify about a criminal investigation, and given my role as a prosecutor, there are reasons why my testimony will necessarily be limited.

First, public testimony could affect several ongoing matters. In some of these matters, court rules or judicial orders limit the disclosure of information to protect the fairness of the proceedings. And consistent with longstanding Justice Department policy, it would be inappropriate for me to comment in any way that could affect an ongoing matter.

Second, the Justice Department has asserted privileges concerning investigative information and decisions, ongoing matters within the Justice Department, and deliberations within our office. These are Justice Department privileges that I will respect. The Department has released the letter discussing the restrictions on my testimony. I, therefore, will not be able to answer questions about certain areas that I know are of public interest.

For example, I am unable to address questions about the opening of the FBI's Russia investigation, which occurred months before my appointment, or matters related to the so-called "Steele Dossier." These matters are the subject of an ongoing review by the Department. Any questions on these topics should, therefore, be directed to the FBI or the Justice Department.

As I explained when we closed the Special Counsel's Office in May, our report contains our findings and analysis and the reasons for the decisions we made. We conducted an extensive investigation over two years. In writing the report, we stated the results of our investigation with precision. We scrutinized every word. I do not intend to summarize or describe the results of our work in a different way in the course of my testimony today. As I said on May 29: the report is my testimony. And I will stay within that text.

And as I stated in May, I also will not comment on the actions of the Attorney General or of Congress. I was appointed as a prosecutor, and I intend to adhere to that role and to the Department's standards that govern it.

I will be joined today by the Deputy Special Counsel, Aaron Zebley. Mr. Zebley has extensive experience as a federal prosecutor and at the FBI, where he served as Chief of Staff. Mr. Zebley was responsible for the day-to-day oversight of the investigations conducted by our Office.

I also want to again say thank you to the attorneys, the FBI agents, the analysts, and the professional staff *who helped us conduct this investigation in a fair and independent manner. These individuals, who spent nearly two years working on this matter, were of the highest integrity.*

And let me say one more thing. Over the course of my career, I've seen a number of challenges to our democracy. The Russian government's effort to interfere in our election is among the most serious. As I said on May 29, this deserves the attention of every American."

Robert Mueller's Testimony to Congress

Robert Mueller, in his testimony to Congress, reiterated that Trump was not exculpated. Those who were expecting some new revelations from Mueller in his statement were disappointed. However, Mueller, once again, shed light on Russia's interference in the 2016 elections or President Trump's attempts to mislead his probe and warned about Russian election tampering. He said, *"They're doing it as we sit here. I hope this is not the new normal, but I fear it is."*

In 7 hours of highly anticipated hearings before the House Judiciary and Intelligence Committees, Mueller, who led the investigation into Russia's interference and whether Trump associates participated in it, spoke in defense of his 448-page report that he and his team produced back in April. Mueller repeatedly refused to offer his opinion on critical questions or read directly from his lengthy statement.

However, Democrats managed to get his confirmation on some of the most damaging elements of his findings. When serious questions were directed at him, Mueller said the president was not cleared of obstructing justice in his report. He also confirmed that Trump was not wholly exonerated, either as the president has declared so often. Mueller went on to say that Trump had been untruthful in some of the responses that he gave under oath during the investigation.

Mueller called Trump's encouragement of WikiLeaks 'problematic'. WikiLeaks published the emails stolen by Russian agents during the 2016 presidential campaign from the Democratic National Committee and then from Hillary Clinton's campaign chairman, John Podesta. For those who don't know, Trump cheered the action and urged voters to read the leaked communications.

When Representative Mike Quigley, Democrat of Illinois, questioned Mueller on the president's response to WikiLeaks, Mueller did not mince words. He said, *"It's problematic — is an understatement, in terms of what it displays in terms of giving some hope or some boost to what is and should be illegal activity."*

The former special counsel was frequently responding to questions with one-word answers, like 'no,' 'true,' and 'that's accurate.' However, Mueller defended his work and supported his findings that implicated that Trump was elected with Russia's help. He also cataloged Trump's frantic attempts to undermine the investigation into Russia's election interference. Mueller's statement that ongoing FBI investigations prevented him from discussing if former national security adviser Michael Flynn's lies posed a national security threat also came as a piece of news to the intelligence committee.

"It's not a witch hunt," Mueller said to the Intelligence panel when he was questioned by the chairman, Representative Adam Schiff of California. *"Absolutely, it was not a hoax,"* he went on to say. Mueller further added that the indictments his team brought related to Russia's interference in the 2016 election were 'substantial' and had been 'underplayed, to a certain extent.'

Schiff said Mueller's vague answers demanded more aggressive attempts by Congress to investigate Trump. Schiff said to Mueller, *"You would not tell us whether the president should be impeached, nor did we ask you since it is our responsibility to determine the proper remedy for the conduct outlined in your report. Whether we decide to impeach the president in the*

House or we do not, we must take any action necessary to protect the country while he is in office."

Trump Gave Untruthful and Incomplete Written Answers

Mueller didn't say much about why he did not force the president to sit for an in-person interview during the investigation. He told lawmakers that he opted against issuing a subpoena for Trump so that he could expedite the probe. However, Mueller made it clear that he believed Trump had been dishonest and not transparent in his written responses. When Representative Val Demings, Democrat of Florida, asked if it was fair to say that Trump's answers were incomplete and untruthful, Mueller responded with another one-word answer, "Generally."

Mueller on Indicting Trump

Representative Ted Lieu, Democrat of California and an early proponent of impeachment, asked Mueller if the reason he did not indict the president for obstruction of justice was because of a Justice Department opinion that states that a sitting president cannot be indicted. From the answer that Mueller gave, it was somewhat unclear what he meant, or if he understood the question in the first place.

Referring to the Mueller report's lengthy description of actions that Trump took to interfere with his investigation, Lieu said, "I believe a reasonable person looking at these facts could conclude that all three elements of the crime of obstruction of justice have been met. I'd like to ask you the reason, again, that you did not indict Donald Trump is because of the O.L.C. opinion stating that you cannot indict a sitting president, correct?"

"That is correct," Mueller responded. As it turns out, that response directly contradicted the report itself and Mueller's statement he gave back in May in which he said that he and his team did not decide whether to charge the president because of the Office of Legal Counsel opinions. However, by afternoon,

Mueller took back the inconsistency, saying that Rep. Lieu had incorrectly described his decision. He said, "What I wanted to clarify is the fact that we did not make any determination with regard to culpability in any way."

Trump Was Not Exculpated

Mueller seemed like a reluctant witness who refused to say anything beyond his 448-page report. However, Democrats promoted him to restate some of the most damning aspects of his findings. When asked about his conclusions on whether the president obstructed justice, Mueller told Representative Jerrold Nadler, Democrat of New York and the Judiciary Committee chairman, *"The finding indicates that the president was not exculpated for the acts that he allegedly committed."*

According to The New York Times report, this was one of the rare instances in which Mueller strayed outside of one-word answers or short phrases in response to lawmakers' questions about his investigation.

Mueller's concise responses and unwillingness to go beyond his report did not give what both parties were expecting from the day's hearing. Mueller refrained from giving Democrats new sound bites and declined Republicans' help to undermine the origins of his investigation. Here's one example:

Representative Ted Deutch, Democrat of Florida, asked, "Why? Director Mueller, why did the president of the United States want you fired?" to which he responded, "I can't answer that question."

However, in a carefully constructed line of questioning, Chairman Nadler for Mueller agreed with him that Trump's frequent declarations that the probe had found 'no obstruction' and had 'completely and totally exonerated' were false.

"Correct, that is not what the report said," Mueller said.

Almost everyone was able to notice that the former special counsel stumbled numerous times during his testimony, often asked lawmakers to repeat their questions or seemed not to have heard them correctly, and kept his answers as narrowly focused as he could. In short, his performance invited concerns from some Democrats. For instance, David Axelrod, the strategist who served as a senior adviser in Barack Obama's White House, gently suggested that Mueller might not be up to his task. Here's what he commented on Twitter:

"This is delicate to say, but Mueller, whom I deeply respect, has not publicly testified before Congress in at least six years. And he does not appear as sharp as he was then."

As for Republicans, they treated Mueller as a hostile witness and tried to confuse him with a prosecutorial approach, often intimidating or bullying the former special counsel with specific findings in his report. For instance, Representative Doug Collins of Georgia, the committee's senior Republican, challenged Mueller repeatedly on whether 'conspiracy' and 'collusion' were the same things or not. That prompted Mueller to ultimately respond, *"I leave it with the report."*

Collins also steered his questions to ask something that the investigation did not find. He asked if it was accurate that the report did not establish that Trump 'was involved in the underlying crime of Russia interference.' Mueller gave a very legalistic response: *"We found insufficient evidence of the president's culpability."*

Republicans Took Aim at Mueller

At the hearing, Democrats might have been interested in digging into the details of Mueller's report, but Republican lawmakers were more interested in attacking the former special counsel. They consistently suggested that Mueller's probe was tainted and misguided. The Republican questioning offered the tensest moments of hearing.

Representative John Ratcliffe of Texas berated Mueller for his handling of the investigation. He argued that he had used an 'inverted burden of proof' by choosing to detail Trump's behavior without charging him with any crime. Here's what he said:

"You wrote 180 pages — 180 pages! — about decisions that weren't reached, about potential crimes that weren't charged or decided. By doing that, you managed to violate every principle in the most sacred of traditions about prosecutors not offering extra prosecutorial analysis about potential crimes that aren't charged."

Republicans were determined to prove that Mueller acted in a biased way. Representative Jim Jordan of Ohio went on ranting about why Mueller did not choose to charge Joseph Mifsud, the London-based professor who informed George Papadopoulos that the Russian government had obtained 'dirt' on Hillary Clinton in the form of thousands of emails.

"You can charge all kinds of people who are around the president with false statements, but the guy who launches everything, the guy who puts this whole

story in motion, you can't charge him. I think that's amazing." Jordan said with his voice rising.

Jordan's statement and the manner in which he made it drew a rare challenge from Mueller. He just replied quietly, *"I'm not sure I agree with your characterization."*

The temperature continued to rise in the hearing room as Trump's inner circle persistently discredited Mueller. Donald Trump Jr. said the real Mueller, 74, had been kidnapped and replaced with *"a mentally retarded look-alike."*

As for President Trump, he was slightly gentler but no less sparing in his comment on Mueller. He said in a tweet, "This has been a disaster for the Democrats and a disaster for the reputation of Robert Mueller."

Adam Schiff was completely accurate on March 28, 2019, **'You might think it's okay.'**

My colleagues might think it's okay that the Russians offered dirt on the Democratic candidate for president as part of what's described as the Russian government's effort to help the Trump campaign.

You might think that's okay. My colleagues might think it's okay that when that was offered to the son of the president, who had a pivotal role in the campaign, the president's son did not call the FBI, he did not adamantly refuse that foreign help — no, instead that son said he would 'love' the help with the Russians. You might think it was okay that he took that meeting. You might think it's okay that Paul Manafort, the campaign chair, someone with great experience running campaigns, also took that meeting. You might think it's okay that the president's son-in-law also took that meeting. You might think it's okay that they concealed it from the public. You might think it's okay that their only disappointment after that meeting was that the dirt, they received on Hillary Clinton wasn't better. You might think it's okay. I don't.

You might think it's okay that, when it was discovered a year later that they had lied about that meeting and said it was about adoptions, you might think it's okay that the president is reported to have helped dictate that lie. You might think it's okay. I don't.

You might think it's okay that the campaign chairman of a presidential campaign would offer information about that campaign to a Russian oligarch in exchange for money or debt forgiveness. You might think that's okay. I don't. You might think it's okay that that campaign chairman offered polling data, campaign polling data, to someone linked to Russian intelligence. I don't think that's okay.

You might think it's okay if that the president himself called on Russia to hack his opponent's emails; if they were listening. You might think it's okay that, later that day, the Russians, in fact, attempted to hack a server affiliated with that campaign. I don't think that's okay.

You might think that it's okay that the president's son-in-law sought to establish a secret back-channel of communication with Russians through a Russian diplomatic facility. I don't think that's okay.

You might think it's okay that an associate of the president made direct contact with the GRU through Guccifer 2.0 and WikiLeaks, which is considered a hostile intelligence agency. You might think it's okay that a senior campaign official was instructed to reach that associate and find out what that hostile intelligence agency had to say, in terms of dirt on his opponent.

You might think it's okay that the national security adviser-designate secretly conferred with a Russian ambassador about undermining U.S. sanctions, and you might think it's okay he lied about it to the FBI. You might say that's all okay. You might say that's just what you need to do to win. But I don't think it's okay. I think it's immoral, I think it's unethical, I think it's unpatriotic, and, yes, I think it's corrupt, and evidence of collusion.

Now, I have always said that whether this amounts to proof of conspiracy was another matter. Whether the special counsel could prove beyond a reasonable doubt the proof of that crime was up to the special counsel and that I would accept his decision, and I do. He is a good and honorable man, and he is a good prosecutor. But I do not think that conduct, criminal or not, is okay. And the day we do think that's okay is the day we will look back and say, that is the day America lost its way.

And I'll tell you one more thing that is the purpose of the hearing today. I don't think it's okay that during a presidential campaign Mr. Trump sought the Kremlin's help to consummate a real estate deal in Moscow that would make him a fortune. According to the special counsel, hundreds of millions of dollars. I don't think it's okay that he concealed it from the public. don't think it's okay he advocated a new and more favorable policy towards the Russians, even as he was seeking the Russian's help, the Kremlin's help, to make money.

I don't think it's okay that his attorney lied to our committee. There is a different word for that than collusion, and it's called compromise. And that's the subject of our hearing today.

However, if Rep. Adam Schiff interactions with his GOP colleagues at this moment; he would probably say, *"His colleagues might still think it's okay for the President to continue asking foreign countries to interfere in the US election for his political gain against his opponent former V.P Joe Biden, as he did on the 2016 election against Hillary Clinton."* A new severe storm has begun with the 'whistleblower's full complaint scandal.' Which has been directed to the President's Impeachment and cleared by the GOP senators.

Hence, if President Nixon had a chance that President Trump has today under This GOP generation, he would never resign from his position; for there is unquestionably no comparison between his scandal to Trump's scandals.

Democrats Seek the White House Press for Impeachment

Several candidates vying for the Democratic nomination for president responded to Mueller's testimony. One of the candidates was Senator Elizabeth Warren of Massachusetts. She reiterated that she believes Mueller's report amounts to an impeachment referral and that Congress should initiate the proceedings.

"We have to make clear; no one is above the law, not even the president of the United States. Some things are above politics, and one of them is our constitutional responsibility to do what is right. And the responsibility of the Congress of the United States of America, when a president breaks the law, is to bring impeachment charges against that president." Warren said at an N.A.A.C.P. candidate forum in Detroit. This was a day after the Democrats called on the White House to begin impeachment proceedings against Trump."

Some of Warren's rivals for the Democratic nomination also shared their thoughts. Senator Bernie Sanders of Vermont said, *"We know for a fact that the president did everything that he could to obstruct the Mueller investigation."* He was not surprised to hear that Mueller had testified that his report did not exonerate the president of the obstruction of justice allegations.

Senator Kamala Harris of California went on to say that on the basis of what she had heard about Mueller's testimony, 'there is no exoneration.' She said, "No matter what this current attorney general and the president of the United States try to say, the American people are smart enough to know what is and what is not the truth."

President Trump's Response to Mueller's Testimony

After the hearing ended, Trump emerged from the Oval Office and declared that the White House had a 'very good day.' He also asserted that there was 'no defense of what Robert Mueller was trying to defend.' He added that Mueller did a 'horrible' job in testifying and called the event a 'devastating day' for Democrats. Here's what he said to the reporter:

"This has been a very bad thing for our country. And despite everything we've been through, it's been an incredible two-and-a-half years for our country. What he showed more than anything else is that this whole thing has been three years of embarrassment and a waste of time for our country."

When the reporter asked Trump if he was worried, he could be indicted once out of office, Trump ended up criticizing him and called him 'one of the worst. Trump also defended his decision not to sit for an interview with Robert Mueller. The president said, *"I've seen how they've destroyed people. I did the right thing."*

To this day, Trump refuses to admit that the Russian attack ever happened because that would reduce the greatness of his victory. Will everything go according to the plan for Trump? As it turns out, there are too many constraints built into the system, and there are many ongoing investigations that the president might not be able to outrun.

There's one thing we need to know is being attempted: the GOP has set the stage for an investigation of the investigators. It would do anything in its power to supplant a real crime with a fictional one.

From this, you can see how the GOP leaders completely ignore the moral issue facing this country. They are no longer the defenders of the country's interest, and they don't care about the real concern of the American people. They only care about themselves and completely ignore why the voters send them to Washington. As it turns out, you don't have to be a psychologist to realize what Republicans have done in this country.

You can look at their actions and hear the words they speak to know that most of them are entirely dishonest and corrupt. They never fail to mask the truth to hide it from the American people. Nowadays, this has become the only real reason that people cannot perceive reality beyond a reasonable doubt.

However, after what happened in the 2016 presidential election, which is a travesty, to say the least, Americans will have to think twice before voting. That would be their moral responsibility before casting their precious votes

---·—

BIBLIOGRAPHY

1 3 RUSSIANS INDICTED AS Mueller Reveals Effort to Aid Trump Campaign—The New York Times. (n.d.). Retrieved September 30, 2019, from

  B3-DH044_Exhibi_E_20190227110920.jpg (612×792). (n.d.). Retrieved September 30, 2019, from

  B3-DH046_Exhibi_E_20190227111023.jpg (3024×4032). (n.d.). Retrieved September 30, 2019, from

  Bellefonte Nuclear Plant—Wikipedia. (n.d.). Retrieved September 30, 2019, from

Blackwater founder held secret Seychelles meeting to establish Trump-Putin back channel—The Washington Post. (n.d.). Retrieved September 30, 2019, from

Donald Trump Jr.'s Emails, Transcribed—The Atlantic. (n.d.). Retrieved September 30, 2019, from

GRU (G.U.)—Wikipedia. (n.d.). Retrieved September 30, 2019, from

Guccifer 2.0—Wikipedia. (n.d.). Retrieved September 30, 2019, from

Highlights of Robert Mueller's Testimony to Congress—The New York Times. (n.d.). Retrieved September 30, 2019, from

Italy—Wikipedia. (n.d.). Retrieved September 30, 2019, from

Korea Aerospace Industries—Wikipedia. (n.d.). Retrieved September 30, 2019, from

Respekt—Wikipedia. (n.d.). Retrieved September 30, 2019, from

Rod Rosenstein—Wikipedia. (n.d.). Retrieved September 30, 2019, from

Russian interference in the 2016 United States elections—Wikipedia. (n.d.). Retrieved September 30, 2019, from

Sergey Kislyak—Wikipedia. (n.d.). Retrieved September 30, 2019, from

Sessions met with Russian envoy twice last year, encounters he later did not disclose—The Washington Post. (n.d.). Retrieved September 30, 2019, from

Special Counsel investigation (2017–2019)—Wikipedia. (n.d.-a). Retrieved September 30, 2019, from

Special Counsel investigation (2017–2019)—Wikipedia. (n.d.-b). Retrieved September 30, 2019, from

Switzerland—Wikipedia. (n.d.). Retrieved September 30, 2019, from

United States Department of Energy—Wikipedia. (n.d.). Retrieved September 30, 2019, from

Alicia Parlapiano and Jasmine C. Lee, February 16, 2018. The Propaganda Tools Used by Russians to Influence the 2016 Elections ( )

L. Dara, 2019, State of the Union 2019: the facts about the US-Mexico border,

https://www.theatlantic.com/politics/archive/2017/07/donald-trumps-jrs-email-exchange/533244/

N. Ellen, 2016, Russian government hackers penetrated DNC, stole opposition research on Trump,

G. Andy, 2016, Trump Asks Russia to Dig Up Hillary's Emails in Unprecedented Remarks,

FBI rebukes Clinton but recommends 'no charges' in email investigation,

K. Andrew, M. Mike, M. Barry, 2016,

H. Caroline, 2017, 13 Things to Know About Jared Kushner,

The Moscow Project, 2016, Kushner and Flynn Meet with Kislyak,

F. Amie, 2017, Why Did Russia Send Sergei Gorkov to Meet with Jared Kushner,

G. Adam, S. Michael & F. Nicholas, 2019, FBI Opened Inquiry into Whether Trump Was Secretly Working on Behalf of Russia,

Y. Matthew, P. Andrew, 2018, The Steele Dossier Explained,

K. Eugene & F. Robert, 2017, Trump vs. Comey on What Happened in Their Private Meetings,

Comey Transcripts: Early Russia Suspects and Claims he hugs Mueller,

J. Greg, 2017, Gregg Jarrett: Comey Exonerates Trump – So Much for Obstruction,

J. Greg, 2017, Gregg Jarrett: Comey Exonerates Trump – So Much for Obstruction,

S. Elliot, 2017, Hard Questions: Russian Ads Delivered to Congress,

S. Alex, 2017, An Update on Information Operations on Facebook,

Revealed: 50 million Facebook profiles harvested for Cambridge Analytica in major data breach,

W. Joseph, 2018, House lawmakers take their turn grilling Facebook's Zuckerberg,

P. Ned, L. Jonathan & S. Warren, 2017, Exclusive: Trump campaign had at least 18 undisclosed contacts with Russians: sources,

M. Sara, B. Gloria, & D. Jeremy, 2017, Flynn Resigns Amid Controversy Over Russia Contacts,

R. Gregg, H. Catherine, & U. Cyd, 2019, Mueller files show Flynn under investigation earlier than thought, as brother alleges effort to 'trap him',

B. Rebecca & P. Joe, 2019, Michael Cohen Details Allegations of Trump's Role in Hush-Money Scheme,

Trump's Russia Cover-Up by the Numbers – 272 Contacts with Russia-Linked Operatives, 2019,

L. Thomas, 2018, Chief Justice Roberts Stays Court Order in Mystery Grand Jury Probe,

N. Ellen, D. Karoun, & B. Rachael, 2019, The Watchword Is Transparency: Democrats Ready to Fight for Mueller's Complete Findings,

M. Laura, 2019, Robert Mueller's Report Shows William Barr's Statements Were Incomplete At Best,

L. Bess, 2019, BARR HAS A HISTORY OF WRITING SUMMARIES THAT OBSCURE THE TRUTH,

H. Siraj, 2019, Here's what you need to know about the Trump 'cover-up',

M. Dan, 2019, 'I don't do cover-ups': Trump lashes out at Democrats after canceling White House infrastructure sit-down,

S. Greg, 2019, William Barr is helping to cover up Trump's biggest crime of all,

S. Emily, 2019, Read Robert Mueller's Opening Statement,

H. Julie & M. Mark, 2019, Highlights of Robert Mueller's Testimony to Congress,

Jean Robert Revolus—#12997005 on Professional Ghost Writer | Trello. (n.d.). Retrieved October 16, 2019, from

Russian Hackers Read Obama's Unclassified Emails, Officials Say—The New York Times. (n.d.). Retrieved October 16, 2019, from